Julian B Speck

The ABC's of MS-DOS

The ABC's of MS-DOS®

Second Edition

Alan R. Miller

San Francisco · Paris · Düsseldorf · London

Cover design by Thomas Ingalls + Associates
Cover photography by Casey Cartwright

AT&T is a trademark of American Telephone and Telegraph Co.
Compaq is a trademark of Compaq Computer Corp.
dBASE III is a trademark of Ashton-Tate.
Epson is a trademark of Epson America, Inc.
IBM PC and PC-DOS are trademarks of International Business Machines Corporation.
Intel is a registered trademark of Intel Corporation.
Lotus 1-2-3 is a trademark of Lotus Development Corp.
MS-DOS and Microsoft Word are trademarks of Microsoft Corporation.
The Norton Utilities is a trademark of Peter Norton Computing.
SideKick and SuperKey are trademarks of Borland International.
SuperSpl is a trademark of AST Research Inc.
WordStar, MailMerge, CorrectStar, and SuperSort are trademarks of MicroPro International
Corporation. .

SYBEX is a registered trademark of SYBEX, Inc.

SYBEX is not affiliated with any manufacturer.

Library of Congress Card Number: 87-63228
ISBN 0-89588-493-3
Manufactured in the United States of America
20 19 18 17 16 15 14 13 12 11
10

Acknowledgments

I am sincerely grateful to Bonnie Gruen, editor of the manuscript, for her many helpful suggestions, and to Rudolph Langer and Jim Compton for early direction. Max Weinryb reviewed the manuscript from the technical aspect and made many valuable comments. Other SYBEX staff members who made contributions are Olivia Shinomoto and Dave Clark, word processing; Cheryl Vega, typesetting; and Aidan Wylde, proofreading.

For their work on the second edition, thanks to Cheryl Vega, typesetting; Lynne Bourgault, proofreading; and Ingrid Owen, design.

Alan R. Miller
Socorro, New Mexico
November 24, 1987

Table of Contents

Chapter 10   DOS Command and Program Summary   181

Appendix A   Hints for Beginners   215

The Workspace   216

Floppy Disks   216

Damaged Files   217

Introduction

This book will teach you to use your IBM or IBM-compatible computer and the software, called DOS (which stands for disk-operating system), that makes your computer operate. You do not need any previous experience with computers to understand it, because all the essential terminology and the basic procedures are explained thoroughly with beginners in mind. However, if you already have some experience with your computer, this book includes some very useful tips and will teach you how to use your computer more effectively.

There are many versions of DOS. Some are called PC-DOS and others are called MS-DOS. The DOS sold by Microsoft and included with many computers is known as MS-DOS and runs on a variety of computers. Microsoft also develops the DOS sold by IBM. This version is called PC-DOS and is especially designed for IBM computers. However, there is little difference between the two. Although PC-DOS is designed to run on computers made by IBM, it also works on other computers. For example, I have used PC-DOS on computers made by Compaq and PC's Limited. Therefore, whether you have PC-DOS or MS-DOS and a computer made by IBM or by someone else, you can follow the examples given in this book.

The DOS version number has two parts separated by a decimal point. The first version of DOS was 1.0. However, there have been many improvements since then. The latest version is called 3.30 or simply 3.3. When the number on the left side increases, it means that the new version contains major improvements. Thus version 3 has many more features than version 2. A change in the number to the right of the decimal point indicates a small change. Thus version 3.3 has a few new features not available in the previous version, 3.2, but they are both version 3 and are therefore very similar. Any version 2 or 3 can be used to follow the examples in this book. However, version 1 should not be used. Because 3.3 has many powerful features that are described in this book, you should consider changing to this version if you do not have it already.

For those using a computer for the first time, Chapter 1 briefly introduces the components and operations of your computer. Use of both the 5-inch disk and the new 3.5-inch disk is discussed. If you feel comfortable working with your computer, you can start with Chapter 2, where you learn how to turn on your computer, how to set the date and time, how to correct typing errors, and how to give simple DOS commands.

Chapter 3 introduces disk operations. You learn how to duplicate a disk, how to choose names for your programs, and how to use *wild-card* symbols to reference a group of files. You create a short disk file containing words you type at the keyboard.

Chapter 4 is devoted to the DOS editor, EDLIN, that can be used to create and alter disk files. If you have a new hard disk, you can learn how to prepare it for use in Chapter 5. You can also learn how to make your computer easier to use by programming DOS to do things your way. Several short programs that change the operation of DOS are also included in Chapter 5.

In Chapter 6 you learn how to use the built-in DOS commands TYPE, DIR, REN, DEL, and ERASE. Chapter 7 shows you how to use the DOS external programs ATTRIB, COMP, FIND, MORE, LABEL, and

ASSIGN. You write two one-line programs to help you find your way around a hard disk. Chapter 8 is entirely devoted to the COPY command that is used to duplicate disk files.

The resident utility programs SideKick and SuperKey are described in Chapter 9. When these programs are installed in your computer, you can pop up a calendar or calculator on the video screen while you are in the middle of something else. You can assign special tasks or display whole sentences with just the press of a single key. You can display the date by pressing one key and the time by pressing another. You can recall any previous command, change it, and then run it again.

The DOS commands and programs are summarized in Chapter 10 in alphabetical order. It provides a quick reference when you need details about a particular operation.

The appendices provide additional information. Appendix A gives practical hints about using and caring for your computer. The DOS control characters are summarized in Appendix B and the extended ASCII character set is given in Appendix C.

1 *A Brief Survey of Your Computer*

This chapter introduces you to the operation of your IBM PC or IBM-compatible PC. If you have used a microcomputer before and are familiar with the various components and operations, you can skip this chapter and begin with the next one. If you are new to computers, this chapter will give you enough information to begin working with your computer.

The purpose of a computer is to manipulate information, whether it is a huge NASA computer calculating the path of a rocket or a small computer printing address labels for a social club. This book describes the operation of small personal computers, or microcomputers, sold by IBM, Compaq, AT&T, Tandy, HP, and others. Because IBM was the first company to sell computers of this type, they are known as IBM or IBM-compatible PCs. If they are not sold by IBM they are sometimes called *clones* but they are rarely exact duplicates (as clones should be). In particular, they are missing a built-in program called BASIC. The clones can run BASIC, but it is not built-in. In addition, each microcomputer has built-in instructions for operating the computer. The IBM version is not the same as the others. Therefore, some programs designed for IBM computers will not run on clones. Nevertheless, the operation of IBM clones is so close to the IBM for most purposes that the examples in this book apply to either type of computer.

A computer has two different parts that work together. The *hardware* is the physical part of a computer and includes the keyboard, video screen, printer, and disks. The *software* is the intangible aspect of the computer: the programs and data that tell the computer what to do. We might compare the hardware to a piano and the software to the music written for the piano. A computer needs both hardware and software.

THE HARDWARE

The hardware is contained in several parts. Figure 1.1 shows a personal computer with three parts. The system unit is in the middle, the video screen is on top, and the keyboard is in front. All IBMs and IBM clones have these basic parts. Let us look at these parts in more detail.

THE SYSTEM UNIT

The *system unit* is a box that contains most of the computer. It has the disk drives, the input and output (I/O) ports, and electronic elements such as the central processing unit (CPU) and the main memory. It may also have other accessories such as a battery-powered clock. The system unit performs all the calculations and operates the other parts of the computer. Let us look at the parts of the system unit.

Figure 1.1: *A personal computer*

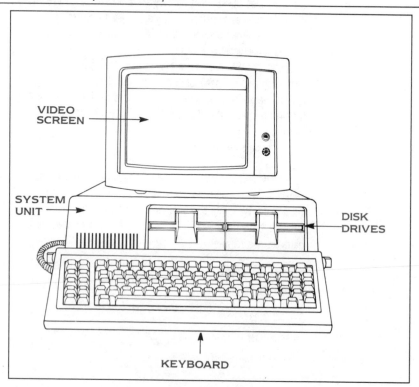

THE CENTRAL PROCESSING UNIT

The hardware element that directs all the computer operations is called the *central processing unit* (CPU). The CPU contains thousands of transistors on a tiny chip of silicon. It can perform many different operations such as adding, multiplying, reading information from the keyboard, and sending information to the video screen. The operation of the CPU is controlled by programs stored in the computer's *main memory*.

The Main Memory

The main memory of the computer is contained in many electrical circuits. The purpose of this memory is to store information including the instructions (called a program) that tell the CPU what to do, and the data to be processed by the CPU. Memory size is measured in bytes or kilobytes. A *byte* represents a single character, such as the letter A. A *kilobyte*, usually abbreviated to K byte or KB, is 1024 bytes and a *megabyte* is 1024K bytes or one million bytes. Microcomputers usually have from 256K to 1M bytes of memory. The main memory is sometimes called RAM, which stands for random access memory.

THE KEYBOARD

When you type instructions at the keyboard, it transmits them to your computer and the computer places the information into the main memory. The diagram in Figure 1.2 shows a standard keyboard, although there are many variations. All have the regular *alphanumeric* (alphabetic and numeric) typewriter keys in the center of the keyboard. However, some of the keys in this region are marked a little differently.

Figure 1.2: *A standard keyboard*

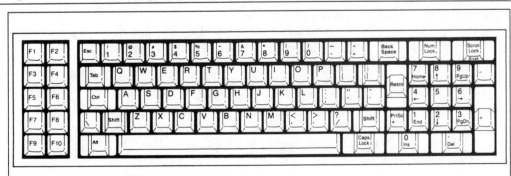

For example, the key marked Retrn in this diagram may be labeled with the word *Enter,* or the symbol ◀┘. No matter how it is marked, the key always serves the same purpose as the typewriter return key: it marks the end of a line. In this book, we will call it the Return key. Another useful key is the Backspace key. On this keyboard, the word Backspace appears. However, sometimes there is only a left-pointing arrow. If it does have an arrow, be careful not to confuse it with the other key that has a left-pointing arrow and a 4 on it. That is one of the cursor-movement keys.

The keys marked Shift on either side of the central part of the keyboard are sometimes marked with an up-arrow (↑) instead and function just like the shift key on a typewriter. The shift-lock key is labeled CapsLock. It works just like the shift-lock on a typewriter plus it has one additional feature. If you press one of the keys marked Shift when the CapsLock is engaged, you return the keyboard temporarily to lowercase.

The keyboard has two other shift keys: Ctrl stands for control and Alt for alternate. When these keys are pressed, they change the meaning of other keys. Thus, each letter key can have four meanings: lowercase, uppercase, control, and alternate. We will use these keys throughout the book. The Tab key, next to the letter Q, is marked with the symbol ⇄ on some keyboards. Finally, there is a key labeled Esc for escape. It is located either on the far right or far left of the keyboard. This key allows you to interrupt or escape from the current task.

Besides the central portion of the keyboard, there are two other groupings of keys. Along the left side are keys labeled F1 through F10 or F12 (on some keyboards you may find them along the top). Sometimes the current definition is shown on the bottom line of the video screen. These are called function keys. The meaning of these keys can change from program to program since any program can redefine them. These function keys can be combined with the Shift, Ctrl, or Alt keys to produce a total of 40 (or 48) different functions.

The right side of the keyboard has a grouping of keys called the number pad that duplicates the regular number keys (0–9) across the top of the keyboard. These keys do double duty; you can either use them as numbers, or you can use them to move around on the video screen. The keys show arrows pointing up, down, left, and right. There are also keys labeled Home, PgUp, End, PgDn, Ins, and Del. The key labeled NumLock selects which of these two meanings you want. If you press NumLock and then the number keys, you will see numbers on the screen; if you press NumLock again and then press the number keys, you will move on the screen. The regular shift keys can also be used to quickly change from one of these meanings to the other. That is, if the pad is set to numbers, you can move on the screen by holding one of the shift keys. Some keyboards have two sets of keys on the right side: one set of keys to move around the screen and one set for typing numbers.

The keyboard contains a separate computer called a processor that keeps track of the keys you press. This keyboard processor communicates with the CPU in the system unit thus freeing the CPU to do other things. Since there is a small amount of memory located in the keyboard, you can confidently type as fast as you want. If the main computer is busy doing something else, the keyboard processor will record the keys you have pressed and send them to the main computer at the appropriate time. If you can type very fast, you might fill up the keyboard processor's memory. Then a beep will tell you to wait until the computer has caught up. If you hold down any regular key for a brief moment, it will automatically repeat.

THE VIDEO SCREEN

The computer lets you know what is happening by writing information on the *video screen,* a device that looks like a TV screen. (This device is also known as a display screen, a monitor, or a CRT, for cathode-ray tube.) One knob on the video screen sets the contrast and another sets the brightness. There may also be an off-on knob. It is a good idea to turn the brightness as low as possible. This makes the images sharper and lessens the chance that the screen will be damaged. (An image that is too bright might become permanently visible.)

When you type on the keyboard, the corresponding characters may or may not appear on the video screen. As explained earlier, when you press a key the keyboard processor sends the corresponding signal to the main computer where it is placed into memory. The main computer then processes your character and either displays it on the screen, alters it before displaying it, or doesn't display it at all. For example, it might alter a lowercase letter to uppercase before displaying it. (Some programs require uppercase letters. Therefore, if you type lowercase letters, the program converts them to uppercase before displaying them.) Or, if you enter the backspace key, the computer will not display a character at all, but instead you will see a character disappear from the screen. The computer can also display information on the screen that you did not type, such as messages that ask you for information or give you the results of a calculation.

There are three different kinds of video screens for microcomputers: a monochrome screen, a color graphics screen, and an extended graphics screen. These screens normally display 80 text characters for each of 25 lines. The monochrome screen displays the regular characters and a limited set of graphics characters, mathematical symbols, and foreign letters (listed in Appendix C). The quality of the characters is very good. The display is crisp and easy to read. Unfortunately, graphics designs such as circles and other shapes cannot be displayed.

The color graphics screen is also known as an RGB monitor. (RGB stands for red-green-blue, the three primary colors used in this type of monitor.) This monitor can produce graphics such as circles and other shapes in 16 colors. However, since this screen is not designed for text, it is very difficult to read letters and numbers on this display. If you need the features of both of these screens, there are two solutions. You can add both screens, the monochrome and the color screen, to your computer. Then you can display text on the monochrome screen and graphics on the color screen. The other solution is to purchase an extended graphics screen, which presents high-quality text as well as color graphics shapes. However, the cost of this one screen is greater than the combined cost of the two other screens.

THE PRINTER

The printer provides a permanent record of operation. Three types of printers are available for the PC: dot matrix, daisy wheel, and laser. The dot matrix is the cheapest and fastest and can create characters of various sizes and shapes. However, the characters do not look as well formed as those from the other two because the daisy wheel and laser printers display very high quality characters. With a daisy wheel printer, however, it is difficult to change the character size and shape. The laser printer can reproduce text of all shapes and sizes as well as graphics. Its disadvantage is that it is quite expensive. It is possible to attach all three of these printers simultaneously and automatically switch from one to the other.

THE DISKS

Most of the memory in a computer is *volatile*—that is, the information in the memory is lost each time the computer is turned off. In addition, memory size is limited. Therefore, copies of programs and data must be stored on a more permanent medium such as a magnetic disk. There are three types of disks: floppy, hard, and RAM. All personal computers have at least one floppy disk. When the computer needs information stored on a disk, it copies or *loads* the information from the disk into its main memory. This doesn't mean that the information is removed from the disk. Rather, a copy of the information is placed into memory. In effect, the computer temporarily memorizes the information. The original version is still present on the disk. The disks are usually housed in the system unit. However, it is also possible to have disks in a separate box that is connected to the system unit. Let us look at the details of a floppy disk.

The Floppy Disk

It is unfortunate that the term floppy disk can refer either to the disk drive or the floppy disk that is placed into the drive. Therefore, we will use the terms disk drive and floppy disk where there is the possibility of confusion. A disk contains a disk-shaped substrate coated with a magnetic oxide film. There are two types of IBM floppy disks—the larger is 5.25 inches wide (called 5-inch in this book) and is shown in Figure 1.3. The smaller is 3.5 inches wide and is shown in Figure 1.4. The disk is protected by an outer container or envelope. When the disk is in

Figure 1.3: *A five-inch floppy disk*

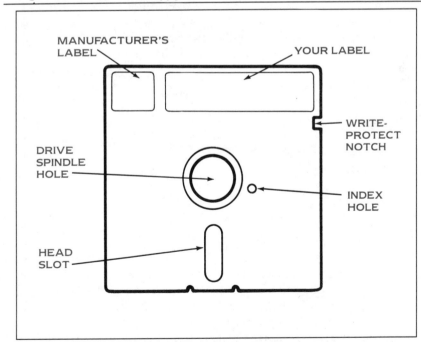

use, it rotates within its envelope. The drive-spindle hole allows the disk
drive motor to rotate the magnetic disk.

The head slot in the envelope for the 5-inch disk allows the magnetic head to contact the disk surface and read information from or write
information onto the surface. The head slot for the 3.5-inch disk is automatically covered by a shutter when the disk is removed from the drive.
The recording and playback of information is very similar to the system
used for audio and video recording with magnetic tape. Disk drives have
two heads, one for each side of the disk surface.

An index hole in the disk surface is used to determine the orienta-
tion of the disk. The rotating disk interrupts a light beam projecting
through the index hole and the corresponding holes in the disk envelope.
This way, the computer can determine the exact position of the disk.

Information is recorded on the disk surface along concentric circles
called *tracks,* which are partitioned into smaller regions called *sectors*
(see Figure 1.5). The regular five-inch disk is soft-sectored, double-sided,
and double-density; it has 40 tracks. The PC AT needs quad-density or

Figure 1.4: *A 3.5-inch floppy disk*

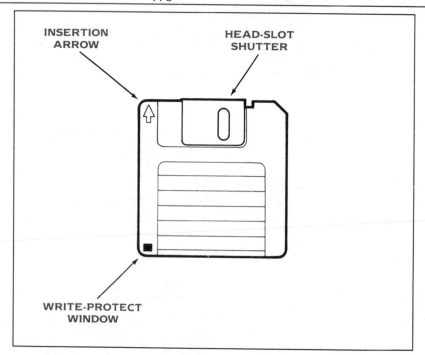

INSERTION
ARROW

HEAD-SLOT
SHUTTER

WRITE-PROTECT
WINDOW

high-density floppies; it has 80 tracks. The 3.5-inch disk has 40 or 80 tracks with either 9 or 18 sectors per track.

Write Protection   Five-inch disks are equipped with a *write-protect* notch (see Figure 1.3). When this notch is covered with a piece of tape, the disk drive can no longer record or write on the disk. However, when the notch is exposed, that is, when the tape is not in place, the disk can be written on. By contrast, the 3.5-inch disk has a write-protect window with a built-in tab. When the window is closed with the tab, information can be written on the disk. When the window is open, the disk is write- protected. Write-protection safeguards important information. For example, the original disks that came with your computer should be write-protected. Of course, you must not write-protect a disk when you want to record information on it.

Aluminum tape for write-protection is provided with boxes of new five-inch disks. Do not use ordinary tape. It is important to understand that write-protecting a disk does not prevent you from using (or *reading*) the programs or data on that disk.

Figure 1.5: *The tracks and sectors of a disk surface*

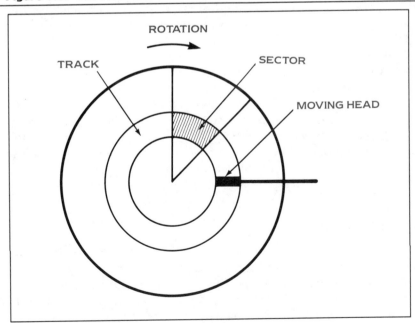

Handling Disks   Five-inch disks are delicate and can be easily damaged. Always treat them with care. Put each disk in its protective sleeve and place it into a box when you're not using it. You can grasp a disk by its outer cover, but do not touch the exposed magnetic surfaces, especially the slotted opening for the magnetic heads. The grease from your fingers can ruin both the disk and the drive head that contacts the disk surface. Do not expose a disk to dust, smoke, or liquids, and be especially careful to keep the disk away from magnetic fields or metal that might be magnetized. Do not write on a 5-inch disk with a ball-point pen or a pencil because the impression of the writing instrument can damage the underlying surface. Mark the disk only with a felt-tipped pen or write on a separate label and then affix the label to the disk. Do not use ordinary tape. Read Appendix A for more suggestions on handling disks.

By contrast, 3.5-inch disks are much more rugged than 5-inch disks. As we have seen, the head slot is automatically covered when the disk is removed from a drive. Furthermore, the outer envelope is rigid. Therefore, there is less danger of accidentally bending the disk.

Inserting a Disk into the Disk Drive   Since a 5-inch disk is square, it can be inserted into the disk drive eight different ways. However, only one way is correct. Hold the disk with your right thumb on the label as you insert it into the drive. The write-protect notch is on the left side. Insert the 3.5-inch disk with the arrow on the upper-left side pointing inward. When the five-inch disk is in position, turn or press the drive handle to close the drive and position the magnetic heads. The 3.5-inch disk is automatically seated. If you are practicing for the first time, use a new disk rather than a disk with important information on it.

You should never remove or insert a disk or turn off the computer when the computer is reading or writing on the disk. There is an indicator or activity light on each drive that is lighted when the disk is in use. To be safe, always check that the light is off before inserting or removing a disk or turning off the computer. You can, however, safely turn off the computer while a disk is still in the drive if the computer is not using that drive.

The Hard Disk

Regular five-inch floppy disks can store about 360K bytes of information and the PC AT can store over a million bytes. However, the typical user might have over ten million bytes of information. Therefore, a larger disk is desirable. Such a disk is known as a hard disk or fixed disk. A hard disk can store as much as 20, 40, or 80 million bytes and operates much faster than a floppy disk. Information is stored on a rigid metal disk coated with a magnetic oxide. The magnetic head can be positioned more precisely on a rigid metal disk than it can on a floppy disk. Thus the hard disk can rotate faster and store more information. Of course, hard disks also cost more than floppy disk drives.

When you are working with a hard disk, you must remember that all the stored information could be accidently erased. Therefore, it is important to make backup copies of important information onto floppy disks. So, even if you have a hard disk, you should regularly use floppy disks for backing up important information. (Refer to the XCOPY program in Chapter 10.)

The first time you start up a brand new computer that has a hard disk, you must use a floppy disk that contains DOS. Then you must prepare the surface of the hard disk. (The procedure is given in Chapter 5.) However, normally when you start up a computer that has a hard disk, you do not want to have floppy disks in the drives. If you do, DOS will look for its programs on the floppy disk rather than the hard disk.

The RAM Disk

A RAM disk, also known as a virtual disk, provides another way to speed up operation for less cost than a hard disk. There is a computer program, described later, that allocates a part of the main memory (RAM) to be treated like a disk. The disadvantage of the RAM disk is that the amount of working memory is correspondingly reduced. Furthermore, all information in the RAM disk is lost each time the computer is turned off. Nevertheless, for programs such as WordStar that refer back and forth to the disk, a RAM disk can greatly speed up your work. We will discuss creating a RAM disk in Chapter 5.

THE INPUT AND OUTPUT PORTS

The computer communicates with the peripherals (the keyboard, video screen, disks, and printer) through a device known as a *port*. Each peripheral is assigned two or more ports for its exclusive use. Furthermore, ports can be one of two types: parallel or serial. Most peripherals use parallel ports. However, some printers use a parallel port while other printers use serial ports. You should not plug a parallel printer into a serial port and vice versa. If you do, both the printer and the port can be damaged.

THE SURGE SUPPRESSOR

There is another important piece of hardware you should have for successful computer operation: a surge suppressor. The electricity supplied to your computer should be 120-volt alternating current with a frequency of 60 hertz (cycles/second). However, sometimes there are higher frequencies generated by other electrical appliances nearby. These higher frequencies will not harm your computer. However, they may cause errors in the recording of information on disks.

A more serious problem is a voltage spike caused by lightning or by turning a heavy appliance on or off. This can subject your computer to a voltage much higher than the design value and so it can burn out components of your computer.

Both of these problems—high frequency and a voltage spike—can be prevented with a surge suppressor. You plug the surge suppressor into the electrical outlet and then you plug your computer and its accessories into the surge suppressor. Leave the computer and peripheral switches on so you can turn your computer on an off with the suppressor. Some suppressors cost less than $10 and others are nearer $100. However, it is possible to obtain a very good one for around $50 from electronic supply or computer stores.

THE SOFTWARE

A computer needs a set of instructions, called a *program,* to make it operate properly. The program is installed in the main memory (RAM) of the computer. Once installed, the program directs the computer to perform specific operations. Computer programs, and any data needed by the programs, are called *software.* Software can be divided into three basic categories: system software, applications software, and data. Let us look at each of these.

SYSTEM SOFTWARE

System software can be divided into two parts: the *operating system* and the utility programs. The operating system runs the computer while the utility programs do special tasks such as preparing disks, comparing disks, and creating a RAM disk. Chapter 7 is devoted to DOS utility programs.

An operating system is a computer program that manages the resources of the computer. It reads your commands from the keyboard, displays information on the video screen and printer, and executes applications programs for you. In addition, the operating system does such chores as managing the disk space and the main memory space of the computer. If the operating system extensively uses a disk in its work, it is known as a *disk-operating system,* or DOS for short. (DOS rhymes with boss.)

Several different kinds of DOS are available. One is designed for graphics and two are for mathematical calculations. However, this book is about two general-purpose disk operating systems named MS-DOS and PC-DOS. It is important to know that a program written for one DOS may not run with another DOS even on the same computer.

However, programs designed for MS-DOS will also run on PC-DOS and vice versa. Therefore, we can consider these to be different names for the same thing. If you have an IBM PC, you use PC-DOS because that is what IBM provides. On the other hand, if you have a clone, you probably have MS-DOS because it came with your computer. (I have tried PC-DOS on many clones and it works fine.)

Once your computer has started up, the operating system stays in the memory as long as the computer is running. You cannot run the computer without it. If DOS does not come with your computer, you can purchase it separately.

APPLICATIONS SOFTWARE

You use *applications software* to perform specific tasks. Word processing programs such as WordStar, spreadsheet programs such as Lotus 1-2-3, and database managers such as dBASE III are all examples of applications software.

DATA

Collections of characters and numbers—for example, the names and addresses for a mailing list—that are manipulated by programs are known as *data.* Both data and programs are stored on a disk in logical groupings known as *files.* Files are assigned unique names for easy reference. In Chapter 3 you will learn about file names and how to create and manipulate data and program files.

SUMMARY

This chapter introduced you to the IBM-compatible computer with its PC-DOS or MS-DOS operating system. We described the basic hardware elements: the system unit with its CPU, main memory, and disks; the keyboard; three types of video screens; and the printer. We also discussed disk drives, floppy disks, hard disks, and RAM disks. We briefly explained the three types of software: systems, applications, and data.

In the next chapter you will learn how to turn on the computer and try some simple commands.

2 *Getting Started*

In the previous chapter you learned about hardware and software, including DOS and tips on handling floppy disks. In this chapter you will learn to use some simple commands. You will also learn how to correct typing errors that you might make when you give a command. If your computer has a hard disk and it has never been used before, you may need to prepare the disk surface. The method for doing so is described in Chapter 5. However, whether your hard disk is ready or not, you can start your computer from a floppy disk just as though you did not have a hard disk.

Before beginning, be sure that the various parts of your computer are assembled and plugged into a power source. The video screen has two cords, one carries the power, the other (the signal cord) carries information to be displayed. For all three types of screens available, the signal cord plugs into the back of the system unit. The power cord is either plugged into the back of the system unit or into the surge suppressor. Turn the contrast and brightness knobs on the video screen to the middle position. If the video screen has a power switch, turn it on.

HOW TO GET YOUR COMPUTER GOING

As you have learned, some computers have hard disks and some do not. Those with a hard disk are designed to start directly from the hard disk and there should be no disk in drive A. In the next section, you will learn how to start your computer from a floppy disk. Therefore, if you have a hard disk and you know that it has been prepared for use, you can skip over this next section. On the other hand, it will do no harm to start your computer from a floppy disk rather than the hard disk.

USING A FLOPPY DISK

Before you turn on your computer, place a disk containing DOS into the disk drive. If you have two DOS disks, be sure to use the main one, which may be marked Startup, not the one marked Supplemental Programs or Operating. If you only have one drive, place the floppy disk into that drive. If you have two drives, put the disk into the left one if they are side by side, or into the top one if they are arranged vertically.

USING A HARD DISK

Before you start the computer from the hard disk make sure you do not have a disk in drive A or the computer will not be able to start from the hard disk. If the hard disk is properly set up, the computer will read a copy of DOS from the hard disk. If your computer does not match the operations in the next sections, perhaps the hard disk is not properly prepared. Follow the instructions for a floppy-disk system for now. When you get to Chapter 5, you will learn how to prepare a hard disk.

TURNING ON YOUR COMPUTER

If your monitor has an off/on switch, turn it on. Then turn on your computer's main switch. It is usually at the right side near the back but it may be in front. If all the parts of your computer are plugged into a surge suppressor, turn on all parts, then turn on the switch on the surge suppressor. From now on, always leave the monitor and system-unit switches turned on. You can just switch the computer on and off using the surge suppressor.

One of the first things the computer does when turned on is check its main memory (RAM). Some computers display the amount of memory that has been checked as a rapidly changing number on the upper-left corner of the video screen. (The number refers to the amount of memory checked, in K bytes.) On the other hand, your computer may only show a blinking line on the screen. If all the checks are successful, you will hear a single beep indicating that all is well. If you have more than one floppy disk and you don't hear a beep, check to see that the disk drive with the activity light turned on is the one into which you placed the DOS disk.

After it has checked the memory, the computer copies DOS from the disk into memory and gives control to it. If you started DOS from a floppy disk, you can now remove the disk and replace it with another because a copy of DOS is resident in memory. Sometimes DOS may need to read a part of the DOS disk, in which case a message will appear on the screen telling you to insert a DOS disk.

DOS checks the keyboard for your commands, starts the programs you request, and writes the output to the video screen and printer. Thus DOS becomes a resident part of your computer. Imagine DOS as an ever-present servant ready to obey your commands as long as you are not running another program. DOS always gives control to the running program and all your dialogue is with the running program. When the program is finished, the memory space it uses is released and DOS is started once again.

SETTING THE DATE AND TIME

Your computer has a clock that keeps track of the date and time. However, each time the computer is turned off, the regular clock stops. Some computers have a separate battery-powered clock that continues to run even when the power is turned off. Then a special computer program can copy the date and time from the battery-powered clock into the regular clock each time the computer is turned on. However, if your computer does not have this feature, you will see the following two lines on the screen soon after you turn it on:

Current date is Tue 1-01-1980
Enter new date (mm-dd-yy):

(It always starts with the year 1980.) It will use the date shown on the screen unless you give it another value. Therefore, type the date (but not the day of the week) in the form shown. For example, if the date is March 4, 1987, type

3-4-87

and press the Return key. If you make a typing mistake, press the backspace key. Your last character will disappear from the screen and then you can type the correct value.

After you have set the date, the screen shows the value it has for the time. You will see something like this:

Current time is 10:03:25.34
Enter new time:

Type the time to the nearest minute (using 24-hour time). For example, if the time is 1:08 PM, then you should type

13:8

or

13.8

(if you have DOS version 3) and press the Return key. You have now set both the date and the time. You will find it useful to keep the date and time current. That way, when you create new files, they will be marked with the creation date and time and you can distinguish the more current ones from older ones.

If your computer has a battery-powered clock and also a program to read the clock, you will not be asked to give the date and time. If you do not have a battery-powered clock and want one, you can purchase one for less than $100.

TRYING OUT DOS

After you have turned on your computer, DOS has taken control, and you have set the date and time, you will see

A>

on the video screen. If you started from a hard disk you will see

C>

The A> or C> symbol is the system *prompt.* DOS displays this symbol to show that it is ready to accept your next command.

As you can see, the disk drives are named with letters of the alphabet; A and B are floppy disk drives and C can indicate a hard disk or a RAM disk. The drive you are currently working on is called the current or *default* drive and the letter shown at the beginning of the line indicates which drive is currently the default.

On your screen you will also see a blinking symbol following the > symbol. It is called the *cursor* and it shows where the next character you type will appear on the video screen. You can change from one disk to another by typing the new drive name followed by a colon. Thus to change to drive B, make sure there is a disk in drive B and give the command

B:

Then press the Return key. To return to the original drive, type that letter followed by a colon.

TYPING INFORMATION AT THE KEYBOARD

DOS displays its own messages on the video screen as well as the characters you type on the keyboard. We have just seen that DOS displays the A> or C> symbol when you start up the computer. Then, if you press a keyboard letter key, DOS will display the corresponding character on the screen.

When an example in this book shows you what to type, it will usually show only the characters you are to type. The additional characters that DOS displays will not be shown. For example, when it is time for you to type a command, the computer will display the system prompt. If you enter the command DIR, the display will look like this:

A>DIR

However, in our examples, we will only show the characters that you are to type, which, in this example, would be

DIR

Whenever the computer displays the system prompt, A>, you can type a command. After you type the command at the keyboard, you must tell the computer that the command is complete and ready to be processed or *executed* by pressing the Return key. For the remainder of this chapter we will include the symbol <Return> at the end of a line to remind you to press the Return key. However, when you press this key, no symbol is displayed on the video screen. It simply tells DOS to move the cursor down to the beginning of the next line. Remember, DOS will not act on your command until you press the Return key at the end of the line. In the following chapters, <Return> will not be shown, but by then you will not need to be reminded that you must press the Return key at the end of each line.

USING THE RETURN AND CONTROL KEYS

Let us gain more familiarity with DOS by giving it some simple commands. Be sure that the cursor is next to the DOS prompt. Then press only the Return key. Notice that the DOS prompt appears again on the next line. Do this several times and notice how the computer simply repeats the prompt on the next line. You have seen that the Return key is used to send a command to DOS. However, in this instance, no command was given. Therefore, DOS simply repeats the prompt. You have also seen that it is necessary to press the Return key at the end of each *command line.* This tells DOS to execute the line, that is, to do what the command says. But there is an exception.

Certain commands are given by pressing two keys at once: the key marked Ctrl (the control key) and a particular letter key. When you give such a command, only a single character known as a *control character* is sent from the keyboard to the main computer. In this book, control characters are represented by the symbol ^ followed by the corresponding letter. When DOS displays a control character on the screen, it shows the caret symbol. However, many times DOS does not display a control character on the video screen at all.

Because control characters are a special type of command, you do not need to press the Return key after the control character has been typed. Rather, DOS begins executing the command as soon as the pair of keys is pressed.

For example, while holding the Ctrl key, press the I key twice. The cursor moves to the right because this is the tab key. Now while holding the Ctrl key, press the H key twice. The cursor moves back to the original position because this is the backspace key. It does not matter if the CapsLock is engaged when you type a control character. In other words, a lowercase ^ h is the same as an uppercase ^ H. The set of control characters includes the letters (^ A through ^ Z) and other characters such as ^ @ and ^ [. However, not all control characters are used by DOS. The DOS control characters are identified in Appendix B.

Several keyboard keys are programmed to duplicate often-used control characters. Thus, you only have to press one key instead of two. For example, the Return key, which tells DOS to carry out your command, is equivalent to the ^ M character. You could therefore execute a command by holding the Ctrl key and pressing the M key. But of course, pressing the Return key is easier and the result is the same. Similarly, the Esc key is equivalent to ^ [, and we have seen that ^ H is the same as the backspace key and pressing ^ I is just like pressing the tab key.

There are many useful control commands available in DOS. Two commonly used control commands are introduced below.

Stopping a Moving Screen

Sometimes you need to stop information from moving off the top of the video screen before you have had a chance to read it. This is especially true for programs that do not pause when the screen has filled with text. Then the information moves out of sight as it *scrolls* off the top of the screen.

We learned that DOS gives control to an executing program. However, DOS contains many useful routines that can be used by the running program. Thus DOS is able to monitor the keyboard even while a program is running. If a program uses the DOS routine for displaying information on the video screen, DOS can stop or *freeze* the display.

When information is scrolling on the screen, give the ^ S command, that is, press the S key while holding the Ctrl key. The scrolling will stop. Holding the Ctrl key and pressing the NumLock key also stops scrolling. Then, when you want to resume scrolling, press any key. Of course, the screen must be scrolling or the ^ S command will have no effect. Alternatively, you can freeze the scrolling and terminate the current operation by giving the ^ C or ^ Break command.

Engaging the Printer

Normally, the computer sends output to the video screen. However, sometimes you want a more permanent record of the results. A printer can be attached to your computer for this purpose. There are several ways to send information to the printer, which will be discussed in the next chapter. At this point you will learn one simple way to print; this method is useful when you are first learning DOS because it is easy.

If you engage the printer at the beginning of your session, you will have a written record of everything that goes on during that session: the characters you type as well as the responses the computer gives. Of course, the output will also appear on the video screen as usual. If you choose to do this, be prepared for your session to go slowly. Because the printer is much slower than your video screen, the screen must slow its output to the speed of the printer. To engage the printer, type

    ^P

(for printer) or

    ^PrtSc

for print screen. When you want to disengage the printer, give the ^P or ^PrtSc command again.

HOW TO USE A FEW BUILT-IN DOS COMMANDS

As you have seen, DOS remains resident in memory, checking the keyboard for your commands. Several commands are built into DOS and are always ready in memory. These are known as *built-in* or *internal* commands. Let us look at some important commands. (When you give commands to DOS, you can use either lowercase or uppercase characters because DOS interprets them the same way.) At the DOS prompt, give the command

    VER <Return>

and DOS will respond with something like this:

    IBM Personal Computer DOS Version 3.30

There are several versions of DOS. Changes in the whole number indicate major changes and the digits after the dot denote minor changes. If you have a hard disk you should be using version 3.2 or later. The version number may contain three digits such as 2.11. This means that you have the first revision of version 2.1.

If you have only floppy disks you can use version 2.1; however, versions 3.2 and 3.3 are better. The VER command will tell you which version your DOS is. If your DOS is an earlier version, that is, if it has a smaller version number, you should consider changing to a newer version.

Give the command

    CLS <Return>

and the screen will be wiped clean. (CLS stands for clear screen.) Give the command

VOL <Return>

and you will see something like:

Volume in drive A is DOS

or

Volume in drive A has no label

If you have several disks together, it is easy to get them mixed up. One way to avoid this is to write a different name on each disk. DOS also lets you magnetically encode a name, called a *volume label,* onto each disk. The VOL command displays that name on the video screen if one has been assigned. In Chapter 7 we will consider a program that can assign or change a volume label.

Give the command

DIR <Return>

and you will see a listing on your video screen of all programs stored on the current disk. We will consider this listing in more detail in the next chapter.

CORRECTING YOUR MISTAKES

You will probably find, as you are typing in these DOS commands, that you will occasionally make mistakes. You have seen that it is possible to correct the most recently typed character (if you have not pressed the Return key) by pressing the backspace key. You can also use ^H for this purpose. (If you are a good typist, you may find it easier to locate ^H than to find the backspace key.) In addition, you can discard an entire line by pressing the Esc key. This is equivalent to pressing ^[. When you press the Esc key, the cursor moves down to the next line so you can begin again.

To make more extensive changes to a command after you have pressed the Return key, use the function keys. You can use the F3 key to recall your previous command. You might want to do this to repeat the command exactly as before, to make a small change in the command before reissuing it, or to correct an error in your typing. If, after you have typed a command and pressed Return, you realize you need to change it, wait for the DOS prompt and then press F3. The command appears after the prompt just as you originally typed it. You can then press Return again to reissue the same command or you can change the command. Of course, you can press the backspace key to change a character near the end of the line. However, there is a better way to correct a letter near the beginning of the line.

If you pressed the F3 key to get the previous command, press the Esc key to temporarily clear that line from the screen. Now press the F1 key several times. Each time you press the F1 key, a character from your previous command line appears. Of course, if you press the F1 key many times, you will reproduce the entire command line just as if you had pressed the F3 key. If you pressed F1 too many times, you can press the backspace key to undo the effect. Each time you press the backspace key, one more character disappears from the command line. You can alternately press F1 and backspace to move either to the right or the left in the command line.

If we could only reproduce the previous command, the F1 and F3 keys would not be very useful. However, we can also change the previous command by substituting, inserting, or deleting characters. You can change a character just by typing the desired letter rather than pressing the F1 key.

You can add characters to the middle of the previous command with the insert key (Ins). After Ins is pressed, all characters you type will be placed in the command line at the cursor position. When you press the Ins key a second time, the insert mode is turned off. Now you can press the F1 key to continue repeating the characters in the original command, letter by letter, or you can press the F3 key to repeat the remainder of the command. This way, it is possible to add new letters in the middle of the previous command. On the other hand, you can also delete characters from the previous command. If you press the delete key (Del), you delete the next character from the previous command that would have appeared when the F1 key was pressed.

GIVING COMMANDS TO DOS

Let us try out these editing commands. Suppose you meant to give the DOS command DIR (which displays the disk directory on the screen) but typed

DIT <Return>

instead. Because this is not a valid command, DOS responds with the error message

Bad command or file name

and displays the system prompt again.

To correct your error, press F3 to redisplay your last command. You will see the previous command line:

A>DIT

You can correct this command by first pressing the backspace key or ^H to delete the final character, T. Then, type the desired character, R, in place of the deleted character. The command line should now look like this:

A>DIR

Press the Return key to execute the command. This is a valid DOS command so no error message is given. Press the F3 key again to repeat the last command. You will see your previous command:

DIR

Press the space bar and type *.COM. Your command line will now look like this:

DIR *.COM

Be sure to include a space between DIR and *.COM but nowhere else. Press the Return key. The expression following the DIR command is called a *parameter*. It changes the command.

Press the F1 key several times and you will see how the previous command is retrieved one character at a time. You can press the backspace key and the F1 key to see that it is possible to go back and forth through the command line. Press the Esc key to cancel the line.

WHEN SOMETHING IS WRONG

If the DOS prompt is present but DOS does not display your keyboard entries, then something is wrong. Perhaps the computer is busy doing something else. You may have typed the name of a program and the computer is running it. Sometimes you can get DOS's attention by typing ^Break.

Check the disk-activity lights. If a light is on, it means that DOS is trying to read or write that disk. If DOS is trying to read a floppy disk, but there is no disk in the drive, that is the problem. As mentioned earlier, you should not insert or remove a disk when the activity light is on. If the message

```
Not ready error reading drive A
Abort, Retry, Fail?
```

appears, you can insert a disk after the activity light goes out. Then, however, you must press the A key. Do not press the R or F key or you will scramble your disk. Alternatively, you can shut off the computer and start it up again after a few minutes in the usual way.

If no disk activity light is on, you may be able to reset the computer by holding the Ctrl and Alt keys with the left hand and pressing the Del key with the right hand. This action is called a warm start. It is almost like turning the computer off and then on again because DOS is copied from disk into memory once more. However, this method is faster because the memory is not checked this time. (Be sure to remove floppy disks if you restart from a hard disk.) If you had to set the date and time when you first started up, you will have to do it again. Finally, if this does not work, shut off the computer, wait several minutes, and turn on the computer again.

EXTERNAL PROGRAMS

So far we have introduced several DOS built-in or internal commands. The computer instructions that carry out these commands are a part of DOS and a copy of the routines is always present in memory. No disk is involved. However, there is a limit to how many commands can be built into DOS so there are many other commands that are separate from DOS. These are separate programs individually stored on disk called external commands, external programs, or just programs. However, they are extensions to DOS and therefore are often considered to be a part of DOS.

It is important to understand the difference between built-in commands and external programs. As we have seen, the built-in commands are always resident in memory. They are not associated with any particular disk and so they can always be requested. However, the external programs are located on disk. DOS must be able to find the proper disk so that a copy of the program can be placed into memory and run.

If a program is on the current disk, it can be run merely by typing its name. However, if the program you want to run is not on the current disk, you must include the drive letter at the beginning of the command. By contrast, you must never include a drive name with a built-in command. For example, the command

    A:DIR

is incorrect because the DIR command is located in memory as a part of DOS and is not a separate entity on a disk. On the other hand, the program CHKDSK, that analyzes a disk, is an external program. If you want to run this program you must first find which disk it is located on.

Let us run this program. Put the DOS disk in A and make drive A current. Give the command

    CHKDSK

If another drive is current and CHKDSK is in drive A, you must give the command

    A:CHKDSK

This second version begins with a drive name. It tells DOS to run the program from the A drive. Of course, even if A is the current drive, it is acceptable to include the drive designation. It just isn't necessary.

There is a further complication with a hard disk. As we shall see in Chapter 5, it is best to partition a hard disk into several regions called *subdirectories.* Then you must tell DOS not only which disk but also which subdirectory your program is located on. For example, if CHKDSK is located in the subdirectory named DOS, then we give the command

    C:\DOS\CHKDSK

This command includes the subdirectory name after the drive name and before the file name.

We will consider external programs again in later chapters.

HOW TO TURN OFF YOUR COMPUTER

You do not turn off your automobile engine while waiting for a red light to turn green because you do not expect to be waiting long. For the same reason, it is a good idea not to turn off your computer each time you have finished a task. Rather, it is better to turn on your computer at the beginning of the day and turn it off at the end of the day. On the other hand, if you expect electrical interruptions (because of lightning, for example), then it is best to turn off the computer when it is not in use. Therefore, if you are ready to continue with the next chapter, leave your computer running. However, if you are not going to use it for a while, turn it off.

When you want to turn off the computer, check the drive activity lights to make sure that DOS is not using one of the disks. Otherwise, you can damage the disk and lose information stored on it. When the activity lights are off, you can safely shut off the computer with the same switch you used to turn it on. You can leave floppy disks in the drives, or take them out and put them away. If you have a hard disk, be sure to remove the floppy disks before starting the next time.

SUMMARY

In this chapter you learned how to start up your computer and how to set the date and time. Then you learned how to use the DOS control characters that freeze a moving screen, engage the printer, and correct mistakes. You gave several built-in commands to DOS and learned the difference between built-in commands and external programs. In the next chapter, you will learn more about DOS.

3. Working with Disks and Files

In this chapter you will expand your knowledge of DOS to include the organization of the disks. You will learn how to copy disks, choose a file name, and use wild-card symbols in file names. You will also learn how to display a text file on the video screen and the printer.

WHAT IS THE SYSTEM DISK?

When you purchased DOS, you received a loose-leaf book that is more like a dictionary than a guide. That is, you use it to check the details of a DOS command you already know about. However, it is not very useful for learning about DOS when you are a beginner. Inside the back cover of the DOS manual are pockets containing 5-inch DOS disks and perhaps a 3.5-inch disk. One disk has programs you need often. The other, marked Supplemental Programs, contains auxiliary programs that are less important. Alternatively, the two disks might be labeled Startup and Operating. You should not use these disks in your day-to-day work, because they might become damaged. Instead, you should make back-up copies and use only the copies. Another reason to make your own copies is that there are many programs on these disks that you may never use. Therefore, it is better to create your own special version of a DOS disk that contains only the programs you use often. This is called your *system disk.* (The following sections explain how to make these copies.)

Your system disk is your most important disk because it contains the DOS routines you need to start up and run your computer. If you do not have a hard disk, you will need your system disk each time you turn on your computer. If you have a hard disk, you need the system disk just once to start up your computer and configure your hard disk the first time. After you copy all the DOS routines to your hard disk, it becomes your system disk. You should keep your floppy system disk in case something happens to your hard disk, and it becomes unusable. A hard disk "crash" is not very common. But when it does occur, you must start over using your floppy system disk.

In Chapter 5 you will write some special instructions to DOS so it will always be prepared to do things the way you like. Then your system disk will be different from those used on other computers. However, for now you will use the generic form of DOS.

HOW TO COPY
YOUR SYSTEM DISK WITH DISKCOPY

In this section you will duplicate your main DOS disk. Then you can put the original disk away in a safe place and only use the copy. You will use a program called DISKCOPY.COM that is found on the main DOS disk. This program can easily duplicate floppy disks on any type of system. It is especially useful when you only have one drive although it can also be used with computers that have more than one drive. You must not use DISKCOPY for a hard disk.

USING ONE DRIVE

1. Prepare a new floppy disk by writing the words DOS MAIN on a label. (Labels are included with new disks.) Fasten the label to the upper-right corner of the new 5-inch disk (taking care not to cover the write-protect notch), or at the bottom of a 3.5-inch disk.

2. Place the original DOS disk (the operating disk) into drive A. Give the command

   DIR DISKCOPY.COM

   to make sure that this disk includes the copy program. Be sure to place a space between the word DIR and the word DISK-COPY.COM, but nowhere else. (DOS requires a space between words just as the English language does). Also, don't forget to press the Return key at the end of the line. You will see several lines on your screen.

3. Look at the next-to-last line on the video screen. If it says

   File not found

   the DISKCOPY program is not present on this disk. Check to see that you have the main system disk in drive A. If DOS finds the program, it displays a message like this:

   DISKCOPY COM 6224 11-17-87 12:00p

4. Now run the copying program by giving the command

   DISKCOPY A: A:

   Be sure to place a space in front of each A:, but nowhere else. When you press Return, DOS copies this program into memory and gives it control. DISKCOPY displays the following message:

   Insert SOURCE diskette in drive A:
   Press any key when ready . . .

The program waits for you to change to another original disk.

5. If you currently have the disk marked Operating in drive A, change to the disk marked Startup. Otherwise, leave the disk in place. The DISKCOPY program now displays a message such as

```
Copying 40 tracks
9 Sectors/Track, 2 Side(s)
```

All of the information on the original disk will be copied into main memory if there is room. Otherwise, as much as possible will be copied. Then the following message appears:

```
Insert TARGET diskette in drive A:
Press any key when ready . . .
```

6. Remove the original disk and insert the new one that you prepared in step 1. Be sure not to insert a disk with programs on it since the next step erases any information that may already be on the disk.

7. Press the Return key to continue the process. The DISKCOPY program copies the information from memory to your new disk. The following message appears on the screen if your disk has not been used previously:

```
Formatting while copying
```

If your memory is large enough so that the whole disk can be copied into memory at one time, the process is now finished. Skip to step 10. However, if your memory is too small and there is still more information to be copied, you will see the following message:

```
Insert SOURCE diskette in drive A:
Press any key when ready . . .
```

8. Remove the new disk and insert the original.

9. Press the Return key. DISKCOPY copies more of the original disk into memory and then displays the message

```
Insert TARGET diskette in drive A:
Press any key when ready . . .
```

so you can change back to the new disk. Continue in this way, alternating the original disk and the new disk.

10. When you see the message

    Copy another diskette (Y/N)?

    you know that the copying process is complete. Put the original disk away in a safe place. The new disk in drive A has the DOS programs on it. If you want to make copies of additional disks go back to step 1. Otherwise just press N to terminate the program.

From now on, use the new copy of the system disk that you just made.

USING TWO DRIVES

The method given in the previous section for duplicating disks will work with any computer. However, if you have two floppy drives, it is more convenient to use both drives when making copies. That way, you don't have to change back and forth between the original disk and the new disk. If you do not have two floppy drives, skip on to the next section.

To duplicate a disk with the DISKCOPY program when you have two floppy drives, follow these steps:

1. Put the main system disk in drive A.

2. Write a name on a label that will remind you of the contents. Then fasten the label to the upper-right corner of a new 5-inch disk, or the bottom of a 3.5-inch disk.

3. Put the new disk in drive B.

4. Make drive A current with the command

    A:

5. Give the command

    DISKCOPY A: B:

    to start the copy program. Be sure to put a space in front of A: and B:, but nowhere else. This command directs the DISKCOPY program to copy the disk in drive A over to the disk in drive B.

You will see the following message on your screen:

```
Insert SOURCE diskette in drive A:
Insert TARGET diskette in drive B:
Press any key when ready . . .
```

6. If you started with the Operating disk, change to the Startup disk. Otherwise, leave your system disk in A because it is the one you want to copy. Press the Return key. The program writes something like

```
Copying 40 tracks
9 Sectors/Track, 2 Side(s)
```

on the screen. Now, no matter how small your memory is, the duplication process takes place without your attention. The DISKCOPY program alternately copies into memory as much information as possible from the original disk. Then it copies the information to the new disk. When the copying is complete, the message

```
Copy another diskette (Y/N)?
```

appears.

7. Type N if you are finished. Otherwise, replace the original disk in drive A with another disk to be copied. Then, replace the new disk in drive B with another new one and type Y.

HOW TO COPY
YOUR SYSTEM DISK USING FORMAT AND COPY

The DISKCOPY method should only be used to duplicate your DOS disks when you are first learning how to run your computer, or if you only have one drive. In general, it is better to use the FORMAT and COPY method. Although there are more steps to this method, it has several advantages over the DISKCOPY method. You can give your disk a label or name that is magnetically written into the directory of the disk. (If all your disks have names, there is less likelihood that you will get them mixed up.) This method also arranges the information on the new disk in a more efficient manner so DOS can read the disk more rapidly. Finally, you can select whether or not the DOS system is to be placed on the new disk.

THE FORMAT PROGRAM

In this section you will use the FORMAT program to prepare the magnetic surface of a new disk. You will also place three DOS system programs on the disk.

Before you can write information onto a new disk, you must prepare the surface so it contains a magnetic pattern that your particular computer can understand. This step is called *formatting*. The DISK-COPY program we used in the previous section automatically wrote this pattern on the new disk if it was not present. However, if you use the format and copy method, you must prepare the surface by running a separate program called FORMAT.COM. The formatting program is located on your DOS system disk. You only need to format a disk once. However, it does no harm to format a disk more than once.

To format a disk you must first locate the formatting program:

1. Place the original system disk in drive A.

2. If the prompt is not A>, make drive A current with the command

   A:

   Don't forget to press the Return key.

3. Give the command

   DIR FORMAT.COM

   to check the directory of this disk for the format program. Be careful to put a space between the word DIR and the word FORMAT.COM, but nowhere else. Also, don't forget to press the Return key at the end of the line. DOS will respond with several lines.

4. If the next-to-last line on the video screen is

   File not found

   DIR could not find the FORMAT program on this disk. Check to see that you have your system disk in drive A. On the other hand, if DIR has found the program, the following message appears, indicating that the formatting program is present:

   FORMAT COM 9398 1-01-86 9:39a

If the formatting program is present, you can start it up. But first you must check a few things.

The formatting program will destroy any information previously recorded on the disk. Therefore, be sure to use a new disk or one that does not contain information you want to keep. Be careful not to format your system disk accidentally. The formatting process has two stages to reduce the likelihood of formatting the wrong disk. First, the formatting program is copied into memory and started up. Then it waits for you to change disks. When you have the proper disks in place, you can tell the program to begin. The command you give to start the formatting program depends on how many disk drives you have.

Using One Drive

The method described in this section can be used to format a disk on any type of computer no matter how many drives you have. However, if you have only one drive, you must use this method.

1. Perform steps 1–4 in the previous section to ensure that the formatting program is on the disk in drive A.

2. Give the command

    FORMAT A:/V/S

    and DOS will copy the formatting program into memory. Be sure to place a space between FORMAT and A:, but nowhere else. This command does two things. The first word, FORMAT, tells DOS to run the formatting program. The remainder of the line gives information to the formatting program: the A: tells the formatting program to prepare the disk located in drive A, the /S symbol specifies a system disk (/S is called a *switch*), and the /V symbol says you want to choose a label or volume name (/V is another switch). Switches can be placed immediately after the previous word without a space. A volume name on a disk is like a name on a filing folder. It reminds you of the contents. If you omit the /V switch, there will be no name assigned to the disk.
    After DOS loads the formatting program into memory, it gives control to it. However, the formatting program does

not begin formatting yet. First, it displays a message such as the following:

```
Insert new diskette for drive A:
and strike ENTER when ready
```

It then waits for your command. This gives you a chance to change disks. Remember, DOS has loaded the format program into memory and given control to it. Thus, this message was sent by the formatting program, which is now waiting for your response. That is why you can safely take the system disk out of drive A.

3. Remove the system disk from drive A and replace it with a new disk.

4. Press the Return key to start the formatting process. You will see the message:

```
Formatting...
```

displayed and you may hear a clanking sound as the information is written on the new disk. After a few minutes, the clanking sound stops and the following message appears:

```
Format complete
System transferred
Volume label (11 characters, ENTER for none)?
```

The formatting program wants you to specify the volume name (the disk name) that will be magnetically encoded onto the new disk. The name is optional, but if you do not give one now, you can do it later with the LABEL program.

5. Type the label you want to assign to this disk. It may be any name of 11 or fewer characters, including hyphens, underlines, and spaces, that will help remind you of the material you will place on the new disk. You may want to give this disk the name DOS MAIN to remind you that this will be your main DOS disk. (DOS can distinguish disk labels from regular file names. Therefore, you can use blanks in a disk label but not in a regular file name.) Remember, you can correct typing errors by pressing the Backspace key. Press the Return key when the line is correct.

The formatting program now gives a list of items like

```
362496 bytes total disk space
 69632 bytes used by system
292864 bytes available on disk
```

The first line shows that there are 362K bytes of space on the disk, but nearly 70K bytes are used by DOS (the system) because you included the /S switch. About 293K bytes of space remain on the disk for your use.

Look carefully through the above list for a line that reads

```
XXXX bytes in bad sectors.
```

You should rarely see such a line. However, if this line does appear, it means that you have a defective disk. If it is a new disk, check to see if it is marked for single side or single density. DOS will normally prepare a double-sided, double-density disk. The PC-AT compatible computers use disks that are higher than double density. Some disks are marked quad density, but they may not work with a PC-AT either. You can sometimes use the back side of a disk that is marked as single sided. However, the formatting program may find many bad bytes on this type of disk. Thus it is better to use double-sided disks. If you find the marking to be correct but the disk still cannot be formatted, return the disk for credit or throw it away. The cost of a disk is small compared to the value of information you might store on it.

It is also possible to tell the formatting program that you have a single-sided disk. But then, the storage space is greatly reduced as compared to a double-sided disk. Single-density disks cannot be used.

The formatting program now gives the message

```
Format another (Y/N)?
```

If you want to format another disk, take out the newly formatted disk and replace it with another new disk. Then press the Y key and the Return key. The drive and switches will be the same as for the first disk. Thus, the DOS system will be placed on any other disks you format at this time. The formatting program is still in memory so you can run it without using the disk version. You can continue in this way and format as many disks as you like. If you do not want to format another disk, press N and Return to terminate the program. Remember, you only have to format a disk once, even if you erase the information on it.

Using Two Drives

If you have more than one drive, it is safer to use both drives when formatting. Then you can run the formatting program from one drive and format a new disk in the other drive.

1. Place the system disk containing the formatting program into drive A.

2. If the prompt is not A>, make drive A current by typing

    A:

    Don't forget to press the Return key.

3. Place the new disk in drive B.

4. Give the command:

    FORMAT B:/V/S

    and DOS will copy the formatting program into memory. Be sure to place a space between FORMAT and B:, but nowhere else. This command is like the previous one, but you specify drive B instead of A.

    DOS loads the formatting program into memory and gives it control. However, as we have seen, the program does not begin formatting yet. First, it displays a message like the following:

    Insert new diskette for drive B:
    and strike ENTER when ready

    and waits for your command. This gives you a chance to check your disks. Be very careful that the disk located in drive B is a new disk and not a disk with information on it. Your system disk in drive A is safe if you typed all the information correctly. However, you can remove your system disk from drive A if you are unsure.

5. Press the Return key to start the formatting process. As before, the message

    Formatting...

    is displayed. You may hear a clanking sound as the information is written on the new disk. After a few minutes, the clanking sound stops and the following message is displayed.

```
Format complete
System transferred
Volume label (11 characters, ENTER for none)?
```

6. Type the label you want to assign to this disk and press the Return key when it is correct. The formatting program now gives a list of items like the following:

```
362496 bytes total disk space
 69632 bytes used by system
292864 bytes available on disk
```

As before, check this list for a line describing bad sectors.

THE COPY PROGRAM

You now know two ways to format a new system disk. The newly formatted disk contains the three DOS programs and a volume label. However, it does not contain any other programs. You will add the other programs now.

You can copy all the programs from one disk to another using the COPY command whether you have one drive or more than one drive. However, if you only have one drive, this method is time consuming, and it is better to use the DISKCOPY program described earlier in the chapter. Alternatively, if you have only one drive but you have DOS version 3.2 or 3.3, you can use the XCOPY program. This program is described in Chapter 10.

For now you will use the COPY command to copy the programs from your system disk to the newly formatted disk. Follow these steps:

1. Place your system disk to be copied into drive A.

2. If you have a second drive, place the newly formatted disk in drive B.

3. Give the command

    B:

to change to drive B.

3. Give the command:

   COPY A:*.*

Be sure to place a space after COPY, but nowhere else. Notice that a colon is placed immediately after the letter A. This tells DOS that you are referencing drive A. If you forget to include the colon, DOS will think you are referring to a program named A. Of course, this is not what you want. The *.* symbol is DOS shorthand for specifying all programs on the disk. It is called star-dot-star.

      DOS copies a program from the original disk in drive A into memory. If you have two drives, DOS then copies the program from memory to the new disk in drive B. This process is repeated for each file until all are copied. However, if you have only one drive, the first file is copied into memory. Then you are instructed to remove the original disk and insert the new disk. DOS copies the file from memory to the new disk. (DOS considers your one drive to be both drive A and drive B.) The process continues in this way. You must alternately insert the original disk and then the new disk. After all files are copied to the new disk, the process terminates and the DOS prompt appears.

You have now copied the main DOS disk a second time. It is a good idea to store this second copy in a safe place so that you will always have an extra copy.

HOW TO COPY A DATA DISK

      In the previous sections you learned how to duplicate your DOS system disk by two methods: using the DISKCOPY program and using the FORMAT program and the COPY command. You learned in Chapter 2 that two of the three DOS programs are hidden. Therefore, they cannot be seen in a directory listing and they cannot be deleted from the disk. Furthermore, you saw that the DOS programs use more than 20 percent of the space on a floppy disk. Since the hidden DOS programs are only needed when the computer is first turned on, they are only needed on the system disk. You can put the DOS programs on another disk, but then you will lose a large portion of the disk space. Therefore, you do not want the hidden DOS programs on your regular disks. In this section you will learn how to prepare disks that do not contain the DOS hidden files. We will call such disks *data disks* to distinguish them from the system disk that contains the hidden files. In the next sections you will learn to copy data disks using FORMAT and COPY.

FORMATTING A DATA DISK

Most of your disks will be data disks since you will only need to have DOS on your system disk. The command for formatting a data disk is a little different from the one we used previously.

1. Put the system disk in drive A, and make A current.

2. Write a name on a label that will remind you of the contents that you are about to copy onto your new disk. Then fasten the label to the new disk. Use the name DOS SUPPL for this step.

3. If you have two drives, place the new disk into drive B.

4. Give the command:

   FORMAT B:/V

   Notice that you use the /V switch but not the /S switch that you used previously. This tells the formatting program to ask for a volume label. However, the DOS system files will not be placed onto the disk since the /S is omitted. As before, be sure to place a space between FORMAT and B:, but nowhere else.
   The formatting program displays the following message:

   Insert new diskette for drive B:
   and strike ENTER when ready

   If you only have one drive, remove the system disk and replace it with the new disk. Be sure that you have a new disk and not one with information on it.

5. Press the Return key to start the formatting process. As before, the message

   Formatting...

   is displayed. After a few minutes, the following message appears:

   Format complete

   Volume label (11 characters, ENTER for none)?

6. Type the label you want to assign to this disk (DOS SUPPL) and press the Return key when the line is correct. The formatting program now displays a list:

```
362496 bytes total disk space
362496 bytes available on disk
```

As before, check this list for a line describing bad sectors. Notice that this time the bytes available is the same as the total disk space because the DOS programs are not present.

DUPLICATING A DATA DISK

You have now formatted a new data disk. It contains nothing but the label. The hidden DOS programs are not present because you omitted the /S switch from the formatting command. The next step is to copy all the programs from the original disk with the COPY command. To do this, you can refer to the steps listed in the section on the copy program because the procedure to copy a data disk is the same as it is for a system disk.

HOW TO WORK WITH FILES AND FILE NAMES

Once you begin creating your own programs and collections of data you must give each one of them a unique name. Therefore, let us explore the idea of DOS file names.

Programs or collections of data that are stored on disk are known as *files*. Each file is associated with a unique *file name* that is used to reference the file. When DOS writes a file on the disk, it creates an entry in the disk *directory* to keep track of where the file is located on the disk. Of course, the directory is also located on the same disk.

You can run a program that is stored on a disk simply by giving its name to DOS. DOS then locates the program on the disk from the information stored in the disk directory. The directory of a disk is like the directory of offices in the foyer of a building that lists names and locations corresponding to the tenants of the building. If the directory is destroyed, the programs on the disk, like the offices in the building, can no longer be located.

EXAMINING THE DISK DIRECTORY

Your new system disk in drive A now contains a collection of useful programs. You have already used two of them—FORMAT and

DISKCOPY. You also briefly tried out the DIR command in Chapter 2 and again in this chapter to be sure that the FORMAT program was present on the system disk. In this second example, you gave the name FOR-MAT along with the DIR command:

DIR FORMAT.COM

However, the DIR command can be used other ways. Let's look at one of them.

1. Put your system disk in drive A.

2. Make A the current drive with the command

A:

3. Give the DIR command by itself:

DIR

You will see a long list of file names and other information such as size and date. The first part of the listing is shown in Figure 3.1. You can tell that the files in this listing are stored on the disk in drive A because that drive is identified in the first two lines. You can also see that the name DOS MAIN has been assigned to this disk. If no name has been assigned to the disk, the following message will appear.

Volume in drive A has no label

Each file name is given on a separate line. If you want a printed list-ing of the directory, give the ^ P command to engage the printer and then give the DIR command again. Type ^ P a second time to disengage the printer. It is a good idea to keep the printed version of the listing inside the disk cover for future reference.

DOS FILE NAMES

You can see in Figure 3.1 that each file name in the directory list-ing is shown in two parts. The part in the first column is called the *pri-mary name*. It describes the purpose of the program or file. There can be as many as eight characters in this part of the name. The second part of the file name, shown in column two, is known as the *extension* or *file type.* It identifies the type of the file. There can up to three characters in this part of the name, although there may be none. All command files or programs must have the extension COM or EXE (for executable); files with BAS extensions are BASIC source programs. Files with OVR or OVL extensions are files designed to overlay another file in memory (this conserves memory at the expense of time); help files usually have the extension HLP; and special files that explain last-minute changes to a program are often named READ.ME.

When you create your own files, you must give them a primary name. But they don't have to have extensions. If you do use one, you must choose the extension carefully. You must not use BAK, because it stands for backup files that may be erased automatically. You do not want to use the names COM and EXE because they are reserved for program files. When you name text files such as letters or reports, you do not need an extension. However, extensions such as TXT, DOC (for document), LST (for listing), and PRN (for printout) are useful for identifying your files. Some typical file name extensions are shown below.

ASM	Assembly-language file
BAK	Backup file
BAS	BASIC source file

Figure 3.1: *Directory listing from the DIR command*

```
Volume in drive A is DOS MAIN
Directory of  A:\

ANSI      SYS     1651   12-30-85   12:00p
ASSIGN    COM     1536   12-30-85   12:00p
ATTRIB    EXE     8247   12-30-85   12:00p
BACKUP    COM     6234   12-30-85   12:00p
BASIC     COM    19298   12-30-85   12:00p
BASICA    COM    36396   12-30-85   12:00p
CHKDSK    COM     9832   12-30-85   12:00p
COMMAND   COM    23791   12-30-85   12:00p
COMP      COM     4184   12-30-85   12:00p
DISKCOMP  COM     5792   12-30-85   12:00p
DISKCOPY  COM     6224   12-30-85   12:00p
DRIVER    SYS     1115   12-30-85   12:00p
EDLIN     COM     7508   12-30-85   12:00p
FDISK     COM     8173   12-30-85   12:00p
FIND      EXE     6416   12-30-85   12:00p
FORMAT    COM    11135   12-30-85   12:00p
GRAFTABL  COM     1169   12-30-85   12:00p
GRAPHICS  COM     3220   12-30-85   12:00p
JOIN      EXE     8955   12-30-85   12:00p
       19 File(s)    180224 bytes free

A>_
```

BAT	Batch file
COM	Executable file
DAT	Data file
DOC	Document file
EXE	Executable file
HLP	File with helpful information
INS	Installation file
LST	Listing file
MAC	Macro assembler file
ME	Help file named READ.ME
OBJ	Object file for DOS
OVL	Overlay file
OVR	Overlay file
PRN	Printout file
REF	Cross reference file
SYS	System file for DOS
TXT	Text file

When you select a group of file names, be sure to make the primary name of each file distinct from other members of the group. Do not simply give the same primary name and different extensions or you will lose the backup copies of these files. For example, you could name two chapters of a manuscript CHAP1.TXT and CHAP2.TXT, but you should not name them CHAP.1 and CHAP.2. Let us see why.

When you make changes to a file and then save it on disk, the new version is automatically given the name of the original file. Then the extension of the original file is changed to BAK (for backup). Now, if you first change the file named CHAP.1, the original version becomes CHAP-.BAK. Then, if you change the file CHAP.2, the original of this also becomes CHAP.BAK. Two files cannot both have the same name, so the first CHAP.BAK, which was originally named CHAP.1 will automatically be erased. Thus you lose the backup file for Chapter 1. By contrast, if you name the two files CHAP1.TXT and CHAP2.TXT, they will become CHAP1.BAK and CHAP2.BAK after the changes. Now you have backup copies of both chapters.

In the DIR listings, blank spaces separate the first part of the file name from the second part. However, when you want to indicate a specific file to DOS, you do not type it this way. You may not need to type the extension at all. For example, to run both the FORMAT and the DISKCOPY programs you simply type their primary names. When you do need to include the extension, you must separate it from the first part with a period, leaving no blanks between the two parts. For example, the first file name in Figure 3.1 is shown as

ANSI SYS

but when you give this file name with the DIR command, you must type

ANSI.SYS

Let's see how to determine when to use the full name and when to use just the first part.

Commands and Parameters

You must be careful to distinguish between a command and its parameters. A *parameter* is information given to the command so it will do what you want. You have already learned how to give several commands such as COPY, DIR, FORMAT, and DISKCOPY. The first two of these commands are built into DOS and the other two are external programs; nevertheless, all four are used in the same way. You give the command in response to the DOS prompt. The external programs, FORMAT and DISKCOPY have a second part to their names. Thus their full names are FORMAT.COM and DISKCOPY.COM. However, you do *not* include the COM extension when you execute these programs by themselves. For example, to format your disk you gave the command

FORMAT B:/V

and did not need to include the .COM.

If you use FORMAT after another command, you must include both parts of the name. In this case, it is being used as a parameter, or information for the command, and you type it after the command name with at least one space between the two. (This is why a blank cannot be used within a file name.) Consider the command line you typed earlier to find out whether FORMAT.COM was in your directory:

DIR FORMAT.COM

This line contains two parts. The first part, DIR, is the command given to DOS; the second part, FORMAT.COM, is the parameter. (The symbols /S and /V that you used earlier in this chapter are also parameters.)

As a general rule you do not include the extension for the command or the first word on the command line. However, you use the full name, that is, the main part and the extension, for the parameter.

Valid File-Name Characters

As you have seen, file names should reflect the purpose of the file. They can be made up of any combination of letters and numbers and you can also include the following special characters:

@ # $ % & { } – (minus) _ (underline)

These characters can appear in any position in either the primary or the extension name.

The following characters must *not* be used in a file name because they have a special meaning to DOS, or to some of the DOS programs:

* = + \ ¦ [ ] ; : " , < . > / ?

You can't use control characters in a file name either, because they too have special meanings to DOS. Also, as you have seen, spaces cannot be used in a file name. When selecting a volume name for a disk, however, you can include blanks and other symbols. For example, VER 3-1 is not a valid file name, but it can be used for a disk volume name. (DOS knows that a volume name is not a file name.)

Wild-Card Parameters

Sometimes you want to use a parameter to a command that refers to a group of files. Or perhaps you want to locate one file in a collection of similar files. If all the files in the group have a part of their names in common, you can refer to them with a single parameter that contains wild-card characters. You cannot, however, use wild cards in the first word of the command line.

As you have seen, DOS file names contain two parts, or *fields*—the primary part and the extension. There are two wild-card characters you can use in either the primary part or the extension: the question mark (?) and the asterisk (*) symbol. The question mark represents a single character at the corresponding position. The asterisk refers to all the remaining characters in the field (that is, the primary field or the extension field). For example, if you type a parameter such as

SORT?

DOS matches this name with any file that has the letters SORT and one more character. It will match the names SORT1, SORT2, and SORT3, but it will not match the name SORT12. It will, however, match SORT. This is because DOS considers the fifth through the eighth characters of a four-letter file name to be blanks and a blank character in a file name can match a wild-card character.

When an asterisk is included in a file name, DOS fills out the field with question marks. This is an internal change that is not shown on the screen. For example, if you give the parameter

SORT*

DOS converts the name to

SORT????

Therefore, the parameter SORT* matches the file names SORT, SORT1, SORT12, SORT123, and SORT1234. The result is the same as if the name SORT???? had been given, but it is shorter and easier to type. Let us consider a few more examples.

DOS will fill out the * character in either field of the file name. Thus, *.BAS is expanded internally to ????????.BAS and refers to all files with the extension BAS. The name SORT.* becomes SORT.??? and therefore refers to all files with the primary name SORT no matter what the extension might be. Again, this name also matches the file name SORT without an extension, since wild cards match blanks too.

Notice that an asterisk applies to only one of the two fields—the primary name or the extension—but not both. The special form *.* becomes ????????.??? and so refers to all files on the disk. There can be regular file name characters (letters and numbers) in front of an asterisk, but there cannot be any after it. Thus, the name C*.BAS is acceptable but *C.BAS is not. Recall that earlier you used *.* to copy an entire disk. This was the command

COPY A:*.*

Of course, regular characters can follow the ? wild-card symbol.

The *.* symbol represents all the files on the disk. Wild-card parameters can be used with some programs but not for others. In general, if you want a listing of a group of files, or you want to copy a group of files, you can use wild cards. However, if you want to do something to a particular file, such as change it or display it, you cannot use wild-card symbols.

Try using wild-card symbols with the DIR command to see how you can select groups of files. Remember, the ? symbol will match any one character for each occurrence.

1. Put the copy of your system disk in drive A.

2. If A is not the current drive, give the command

    A:

3. Then give the command

    DIR A∗.∗

    and press the Return key. The names of all files that begin with the letter A are displayed.

4. Type

    DIR S∗.EXE

    and the listed files will include those EXE files that begin with the letter S.

5. Give the command

    DIR C???.COM

    and press Return. The list of names now includes those COM files that begin with the letter C and that have four or fewer characters in the primary name.

6. Finally, type

    ????.∗

    to see a list of all files that have four or fewer characters in the primary name.

If you give these commands on the system disk for DOS version 3.2, the first example, A∗.∗ matches all file names beginning with the letter A. The list includes

    ANSI   SYS
    ASSIGN   COM
    ATTRIB   EXE

The second example, S∗.EXE displays all EXE files beginning with the letter S. The list shows

```
SHARE    EXE
SORT     EXE
```

The third example, C???.COM includes all files with the extension COM and a primary name beginning with C that has four or fewer characters. The file

```
COMP     COM
```

is the only one that matches. The last example, ????.∗ includes all files that have four or fewer characters in the primary name. This includes the files

```
ANSI     SYS
COMP     COM
FIND     EXE
JOIN     EXE
MODE     COM
MORE     COM
SORT     EXE
SYS      COM
TREE     COM
```

You have seen that the display from the DIR command is not typical because there are spaces rather than a dot between the two parts of a file name. The DIR command also uses its own wild card besides the regular ? and ∗ symbols. A blank is equivalent to the .∗ symbols. Thus the command

```
DIR  SORT
```

is the same as

```
DIR  SORT. ∗
```

and so will display files such as SORT, SORT.BAS, and SORT.BAK. The command

```
DIR
```

is the same as

```
DIR  ∗
```

which is also the same as

    DIR *.*

and so displays all files on the disk. However, the command

    DIR *.

is different because of the dot. This command will only show files that do not have any extension. Files such as FIRST, SECOND, and THIRD will be included but not files such as FIRST.TXT and SECOND.TXT.

HOW TO WORK WITH YOUR DISK DIRECTORY

You can see from Figure 3.1 that the directory listing for the DOS disk gives the file names in alphabetical order. However, this happens only because the names were placed in the disk directory in alphabetical order. Usually, however, the file names are not placed in the directory in alphabetical order and you will probably find that the file names are presented in no particular order on your disk directory. Since it is easier to find a particular file in the directory listing if the file names are alphabetical, let us see how to order the list.

USING THE SORT COMMAND

Put the main DOS disk in drive A and type

    DIR *.EXE

to see a list of files that have the extension EXE. The result might look like Figure 3.2. This example shows eight file names. Notice that one of the file names in the directory listing of the DOS disk is SORT.EXE. Files with the extension COM or EXE are external programs that can be executed and you saw that file names should be chosen to suggest the purpose of the program. Therefore, it appears likely that SORT.EXE is a program for sorting or ordering a list of items.

This sorting program is called a *filter*. A filter takes a list of items and changes it in some way. The SORT filter can put a list either in ascending order (0–9 and A–Z) or in descending order (Z–A and 9–0). It can also sort a list according to any part of a line, not just the first part. Let us see how the SORT filter works.

Put the main DOS disk into drive A and give the command

    DIR *.EXE | SORT/R

You should see something like the list in Figure 3.3. The symbol between DIR and SORT is called a vertical bar or fence. On many keyboards it shares a key with the backslash character. The /R switch tells

Figure 3.2: *Listing of files with extension EXE*

```
A>dir *.exe

 Volume in drive A is DOS MAIN
 Directory of  A:\

ATTRIB   EXE      8247  12-30-85  12:00p
FIND     EXE      6416  12-30-85  12:00p
JOIN     EXE      8955  12-30-85  12:00p
REPLACE  EXE     11650  12-30-85  12:00p
SHARE    EXE      8580  12-30-85  12:00p
SORT     EXE      1911  12-30-85  12:00p
SUBST    EXE      9911  12-30-85  12:00p
XCOPY    EXE     11200  12-30-85  12:00p
         8 File(s)    22528 bytes free

A>_
```

Figure 3.3: *Sorting the directory in descending order*

```
A>DIR *.EXE : SORT/R
XCOPY    EXE     11200  12-30-85  12:00p
SUBST    EXE     16611   3-07-85   1:43p
SORT     EXE      1664   3-07-85   1:43p
SHARE    EXE      8304   3-07-85   1:43p
REPLACE  EXE     11650  12-30-85  12:00p
JOIN     EXE     15971   3-07-85   1:43p
FIND     EXE      6403   3-07-85   1:43p
ATTRIB   EXE     15091   3-07-85   1:43p
 Volume in drive A is DOS MAIN
 Directory of  A:\
         8 File(s)    152576 bytes free

A>_
```

SORT to reverse the order of the lines, that is, put them in descending
order (Z–A). This line contains two commands. You have used the first
one before, so you know that there must be a space after the DIR command. The second command runs the SORT program. It does not need
any spaces, although you can place a space on either side of the fence
and before the switch if you want.

You can also tell SORT to put the list in ascending order according
to another part of each line by using the / + switch. For example, give
the command

    DIR * .EXE ¦ SORT/ + 16

You will see a listing like Figure 3.4. As in the previous example, this is a
combination of two commands separated with the fence symbol. The
resulting listing shows the same file names as the previous two examples.
However, in this example, the lines are ordered according to size instead of
file name. The file size begins in column 16 and we used the / + 16 switch.

If you want to arrange the file names according to file-name extension, give the command

    DIR ¦ SORT/ + 9

because the file-name extension begins in column 9. You can determine
the appropriate column number by counting. Try different numbers in
the / + switch until you get the order you want.

USING THE CHKDSK PROGRAM

You have seen that the built-in DIR command lists the names of
each file on the disk along with the file size and creation date and indicates the remaining free space on the disk. You can learn even more
about a disk with the program called CHKDSK. This is an external program found on the main DOS disk. To look at the system disk:

1. Place the system disk in drive A.

2. Give the command

    CHKDSK

The result will look something like Figure 3.5. The first line gives the
total usable space for the disk (362K bytes here). The second line shows

Figure 3.4: *File names sorted by file size*

```
A>DIR *.EXE ! SORT/+16

SORT     EXE    1664   3-07-85   1:43p
FIND     EXE    6403   3-07-85   1:43p
SHARE    EXE    8304   3-07-85   1:43p
XCOPY    EXE   11200  12-30-85  12:00p
REPLACE  EXE   11650  12-30-85  12:00p
ATTRIB   EXE   15091   3-07-85   1:43p
JOIN     EXE   15971   3-07-85   1:43p
SUBST    EXE   16611   3-07-85   1:43p
 Directory of  A:\
 Volume in drive A is DOS MAIN
        8 File(s)    152576 bytes free

A>_
```

Figure 3.5: *Output from the CHKDSK program*

```
A>chkdsk
Volume DOSMAIN       created Jan 1, 1980 12:01a

    362496 bytes total disk space
     38912 bytes in 3 hidden files
      2048 bytes in 2 directories
    303104 bytes in 46 user files
     18432 bytes available on disk

    524288 bytes total memory
    469920 bytes free

A>_
```

that 39K bytes are used by the hidden DOS files and the third line shows how much space is taken up by regular files. The fourth line gives the remaining free space; this number should agree with the value reported by DIR. If there are bad sectors on the disk, they will also be shown in the listing. The last two lines refer to the main memory rather than the disk. The first number is the total amount of memory, the second is the amount available for your programs after deducting the space used by DOS, the printer buffer, and the RAM disk.

You can check another disk by giving the drive name as a parameter. To study the disk in drive B:

1. Place the system disk in drive A.

2. Give the command

    CHKDSK B:

    You will see a display similar to the one shown in Figure 3.5 but with the appropriate figures for your disk in drive B.

HOW TO DISPLAY A TEXT FILE

There are three kinds of disk files—system files, applications files, and data files. You will not need to examine the first two of these. However, you will want to examine data files, especially those that contain text such as letters and reports. In this section, you will learn several ways to display text files on both the video screen and on the printer.

CREATING A FILE FROM THE KEYBOARD

The DOS system disk does not have a text file you can use; it only contains system files. Follow these steps to create your own short text file:

1. Put your working copy of the system disk in drive A.

2. Make that drive current by typing

    A:

3. Then type

    COPY CON SAMPLE.TXT

and press Return. This command line contains three words. The first word is a DOS built-in command. The second word, CON, tells DOS the name of the original file to be copied; the third word, SAMPLE.TXT, is the name DOS will assign to the new file it is going to create. There must be spaces between the three words. CON is a special type of file name that does not refer to a disk file at all. It is short for console input, another name for the keyboard. Thus, this command tells DOS to read the characters you type at the keyboard and put them into a new file named SAMPLE.TXT. (If a file named SAMPLE.TXT already exists, it is automatically deleted.)

4. Type the following three lines:

        This is my new text file called SAMPLE.TXT.
        This is the second line of my new file.
        This is the third line.

    If you make a mistake, use the Backspace key to make the correction.

5. After typing the third line of text, type

        ^Z

    and then press the Return key. This tells DOS that you have completed the file. The DOS prompt will reappear.

You have just created a short text file. Before taking a look at it, let us create a second text file.

CREATING A FILE FROM VIDEO SCREEN OUTPUT

It is also possible to make a file on disk of the information the computer displays on the screen. For example, when you give the DIR command, the directory listing appears on the video screen. However, you can tell DOS to put the information into a disk file, rather than onto the video screen. Then you can incorporate the information in a report or letter. You tell DOS to send screen information to a disk file by using the redirection symbol ">".

1. Put your main DOS disk in drive A.

2. Make drive A current with the command

A:

3. Give the command

   DIR *.EXE >DIREXE

   You will not see a listing on the video screen. Instead, this command tells DOS to create a disk file named DIREXE and place
   the directory listing into it.

   This is an easy way to make a copy of output appearing on your
   screen. You can then incorporate the disk file into a report.
   You have seen that there must be a space between the command
   and the file-name parameter that follows it. Furthermore, if two file-
   name parameters are given, there must be a space between them. However, since the redirection symbol cannot be used in a file name, no
   preceding space is needed.

DISPLAYING A FILE ON THE VIDEO SCREEN

   Now that you have created two text files, SAMPLE.TXT and
   DIREXE, you can inspect them. There are several ways to look at the
   contents of a text file. (Do not use the following methods for system files
   or applications files, those with file type COM and EXE, because there
   will be nothing to see.)

1. Give the DOS built-in command

   TYPE SAMPLE.TXT

   The contents of your SAMPLE.TXT file will appear on the video
   screen.

2. Give the command

   COPY DIREXE CON

   to view your second text file. This is a second way to view the
   contents of a text file. This method is not as convenient as using
   the TYPE command, but it shows another use for COPY.

   Notice that the two parameters are the reverse of the ones you
   used to create the file in the first place. This command directs DOS to

send the contents of the file named SAMPLE.TXT (the first parameter) to the video screen, CON, the second parameter. In this example, CON is short for console output, another name for the video screen. Notice that CON has two meanings: console input (keyboard) and console output (screen). DOS will not let you use CON for a file name.

PRINTING A TEXT FILE

Sometimes you need a printed listing of a text file. For example, you might write a letter to someone using your computer. Let's consider three different methods of obtaining a printed file. There are subtle differences that you will discover as you learn more about DOS. At this point, the first method is the one you should use.

Printing with COPY

You can use the COPY command to send the file to the printer; the command is similar to the one you used to send a file to the video screen.

1. Turn on your printer.

2. Give the command

```
COPY SAMPLE.TXT PRN
```

Your text file will appear at the printer.

The PRN parameter refers to the printer. Notice that while CON can be used for both input (from the keyboard) and for output (to the screen), PRN is only used for output. That is, you cannot send characters from the printer to the computer. DOS will not let you use the name PRN for a disk file.

Printing by Redirecting Your File

Another way to print a file is by redirecting it. Just as video-screen output can be sent to a disk file with the DOS redirection feature, so can video-screen output can also be sent to the printer by redirection. For example, ᵗhe command

```
DIR >PRN
```

will send the directory listing to the printer. Similarly, you can print your text file named DIREXE with the command

    TYPE DIREXE >PRN

Printing with *TYPE*

A third method for printing files uses the TYPE command. You used it previously to get a listing of the directory. This method is not as sophisticated as the other two methods because the commands you type also appear in the printout. However, this method is faster than the COPY method.

1. Turn on the printer.

2. Give the command

       ^ P

    to engage the printer. (You can also use ^ PrtSc.)

3. Give the command

       TYPE SAMPLE.TXT

    Your text file will appear at the printer. The DOS prompt will also appear after the file has been printed because the printer is still engaged.

4. Give the command

       ^ P

    again to disengage the printer.

The ^ P command is a *toggle* that alternately engages and disengages the printer. This method of printing a file is a little different from the previous method where we used the COPY command. The COPY command sent only the file to the printer. The TYPE method sends the DOS commands along with the file. For example, the TYPE command line appears at the beginning of the printer listing because the printer was engaged before giving the command line. You can avoid printing the command line by giving the ^ P command after you type the command line but before you press the Return key.

After DOS has completed printing the file, it displays the usual prompt on the video screen. This prompt also appears at the printer since the printer is still engaged. Give the ^P command again so that no additional characters will appear at the printer.

SUMMARY

In this chapter you became more familiar with DOS disk operations. You learned how to duplicate both a system disk and a data disk using the built-in COPY command and the FORMAT and DISKCOPY programs. You learned the rules for constructing disk file names and the use of wild cards in file names. You studied the disk directory with both the built-in DIR command and the CHKDSK program. Finally, you created a short text file and then displayed it on both the video screen and the printer. In the next chapter you will learn how to use the DOS editing program.

4
The System Editor EDLIN

In Chapter 3 you used the DOS COPY command to create a short text file. This is a quick way to make a small file. However, it is very inconvenient for creating larger files because it doesn't allow you to change the file once you have created it. To help make your file composition easier, DOS includes a text editor program called EDLIN that you can use to create and alter disk files.

Many different text editors are available for your computer, but they all produce the same results. That is, you can create a document with one text editor and then alter the same document with a different text editor. Some of the text editors are easy to learn but not very sophisticated, while others are very powerful but can be difficult to master (and are expensive too). You may have heard of WordStar or Microsoft Word, two popular text editors. These are both powerful editors that can be mastered with some practice. The Sidekick program, discussed in Chapter 9, can also be used to create short programs.

The DOS text editor, EDLIN, is included with DOS. Although at times it is cumbersome and inefficient, EDLIN is easy to learn, reasonably satisfactory for writing a computer program or a short letter, and it is free. If you plan to write letters and reports with your computer, you should seriously consider purchasing a more powerful program such as WordStar or Microsoft Word. Nevertheless, if EDLIN is your only editor, you can use it for most of your tasks.

In this chapter you will learn to use EDLIN. If you will always be using a different text editor with your computer, you can skip on to the next chapter. Before learning the EDLIN commands, let us consider what a text editor is and how it is used.

WHAT IS A TEXT EDITOR?

If you want to write a letter, a manuscript, or a computer program, you need to create a text file and save it on disk. Text files are composed of ASCII characters (the letters, numbers, and special characters) that are coded in a standard way. Since the video screen and printer are also designed for ASCII characters, text files can be readily displayed on the video screen and the printer. However, not all files are text files. For example, DOS executable programs, such as EDLIN and FORMAT, contain binary characters and cannot be displayed directly on the video screen or printer.

After you have created a text file, you may want to make alterations or additions to it. A text editor is used for both the creation and the alteration of text files. When you create a document with an editor, you type the text as you do with a typewriter. The characters you type are displayed on the video screen, but a copy is also placed into a disk file. The resulting disk file can be displayed on the video screen or sent to the printer by the methods discussed in earlier chapters.

When a text editor is used to alter an existing file, the original copy is not changed. Rather, the text editor creates a new disk file based on the original file, and incorporates your changes. The name of the original file is given to the new version and the original file is then saved as a backup copy and given the extension BAK.

The real power of the editor is apparent when you want to make changes to a document. An editor allows you to move easily from place to place in the document. It also allows you to make changes by typing new text directly over the original or by replacing one string of text with another. The editor can help you readily locate a selected passage in the text so you can make changes. An editor will also let you insert text from another file. EDLIN provides all these features.

HOW TO USE EDLIN

To understand better how EDLIN operates, you will now create and then alter a simple file. The various editing commands will be discussed in more detail later in this chapter.

CREATING A FILE

1. Place a copy of your system disk containing EDLIN in drive A.

2. Give the command

   DIR SAMPLE. *

3. Look at the display to see if the files named SAMPLE.TXT and SAMPLE.BAK are present. (You made SAMPLE.TXT in the previous chapter.)

4. If these files exist, delete them with the command

   DEL SAMPLE. *

   (Type the letters DEL and then press the F3 key to reproduce the previous command. This will save some typing.)

5. Give the command

   EDLIN SAMPLE.TXT

   DOS loads EDLIN and starts it up. You will see the message

   New file

   on the video screen, showing that EDLIN is creating a new file name in the disk directory.
       EDLIN has two separate modes of operation: command mode and insert mode. As the names imply, you give commands to EDLIN in command mode and you add new text or change existing test in insert mode. EDLIN begins in command mode by displaying the asterisk prompt. Your cursor is just to the right of this asterisk, indicating that EDLIN is ready for your next request.

6. Give the command

   I

   for insert. You can use uppercase or lowercase. EDLIN responds by moving down to the next line and displaying the symbols

   1: *

   The I command changes EDLIN from command mode to insert mode so you can write text into memory. When EDLIN is in insert mode, a line number appears first, followed by a colon, and then an asterisk. The asterisk is your prompt; it shows you where your next line will go. The line marked with an asterisk is called the *current line*. EDLIN always numbers the lines of your program when they are displayed on the video screen so you can find your way around. However, it does not add these numbers to your text in memory and they will not appear on paper when you print your file.

7. When you see the 1:* symbol, type

   This is the first line of my file SAMPLE.TXT.

   If you make a mistake, press the Backspace key to correct it. The information will appear on the video screen as you type it and it is placed into memory at the same time.

8. Complete the line by pressing the Return key. EDLIN moves down to the next line and displays the prompt again. The new line begins with the line number, a colon, and an asterisk:

   2:*

   You can tell that number 2 is the current line number of your file because the asterisk appears there.

9. Type the following three lines:

   This is the second line.
   This is the third line.
   This is the fourth line.

   Press the Return key at the end of each line. As you finish each line, EDLIN starts the next line with the corresponding line number, a colon, and an asterisk. When you have finished the fourth line, the cursor will be next to the symbol

   5:*

10. Type the command

    ^Break

    by holding the Ctrl key and pressing the Break key. This changes EDLIN back to command mode. Because you are in command mode, the prompt will once again be an asterisk.

LOOKING AT THE FILE

To see what you have typed:

1. At the asterisk prompt, give the EDLIN command

    L

    (for list) and press the Return key. The four lines you wrote will appear on the video screen:

    1:   This is the first line of my file SAMPLE.TXT.
    2:   This is the second line.
    3:   This is the third line.
    4:   This is the fourth line.

    Notice that each line begins with a line number, a colon, and a space. However, these symbols are not a part of your file. Also notice that no asterisk marks the current line. That is because the current line number is 5 but you have not typed any text for it yet.

2. Give the command

    E

    and press the Return key. This tells EDLIN to end the editing session. EDLIN copies the text from memory to the new disk file. The familiar prompt shows that you are back in DOS.
       You have just created a new file. If you want to look at it again, you can't use the EDLIN L (list) command because you are in DOS. Instead, give the DOS command

    TYPE SAMPLE.TXT

3. However, it is not necessary to type all of this command. The last DOS command you used included the words SAMPLE.TXT and you can ask DOS to just repeat it with the F3 key. First type the word

    TYPE

4. Add a space.

5. Press the F3 key and the remainder of the previous command appears.

6. Press the Return key and the lines of your new file appear on the video screen.

ADDING A LINE TO YOUR FILE

Now let's edit the new SAMPLE.TXT file.

1. First bring back your SAMPLE.TXT file by typing the command

   EDLIN

   and pressing the F3 key to retrieve the rest of the previous command. The line now looks like this

   EDLIN SAMPLE.TXT

2. Press the Return key to start up EDLIN. You should see the message

   End of input file

   If, instead, you see the message

   New file

   it means that EDLIN cannot find the requested file. Either you misspelled the name, or perhaps you are on the wrong drive. In such a case, you should return to DOS by entering the Q (for quit) command and give EDLIN the proper file name.
   When you see the correct message on your screen, the cursor should be next to the asterisk, and EDLIN is waiting for your command.

3. Give the command

   L

   and the lines of your file will appear on the video screen like this:

   1:* This is the first line of my file SAMPLE.TXT.
   2:   This is the second line.

    3: This is the third line.
    4: This is the fourth line.

This looks like the listing you got when you created the file with EDLIN. The line numbers and colons are shown. However, notice that this time there is an asterisk at the beginning of line 1 showing that this is the current line.

4. Tell EDLIN that you want to add text to the end of your file by typing

    #I

    The I tells EDLIN to insert whatever you type and the # sign tells it to put that information at the end of the file. EDLIN responds with the new line number, colon, and asterisk:

    5:*

5. Type this line and press the Return key:

    This is the fifth line.

    EDLIN will number the next line (6) and add an asterisk.

6. Type the line

    This is the sixth line.

    and press the Return key. Again, EDLIN will number the next line for you and mark it with an asterisk.

7. Give the ^Break command to leave the insert mode and return to command mode.

8. Give the L command to see your new version. It now looks like this:

    1: This is the first line of my file SAMPLE.TXT.
    2: This is the second line.
    3: This is the third line.
    4: This is the fourth line.
    5: This is the fifth line.
    6: This is the sixth line.

All six lines are displayed. However, no asterisk is shown because line 7 is current.

At this point, the original file SAMPLE.TXT is still on disk and the new version is in memory. If the computer were accidentally turned off (because someone kicked the power cord, for example), the changes you just made would be lost, although the original file would still be safe on disk.

9. To save the new version, give the command

   E

   and press the Return key. This ends the editing session and saves the new version. EDLIN automatically copies the lines from memory into the new file on disk. It renames the original file to SAMPLE.BAK, names the new version SAMPLE.TXT, and then returns control to DOS.

10. To see what has happened, give the command:

    DIR S*.*

    Look for the files SAMPLE.TXT and SAMPLE.BAK in the listing. Notice that the size of SAMPLE.TXT is larger than the size of SAMPLE.BAK, the original file, because you added two lines.

HOW TO CHANGE
YOUR FILE SIZE AND MOVE AROUND THE FILE

Now that you have learned how to create a new file and how to add lines to the end of an existing file, let us see how to make other changes to a text file. It is possible to rearrange or replicate lines of the file. Also, you can search for a particular string of characters or replace one group of characters with another. But before you can make any changes, you must know the number of the line you want to change.

INCREASING THE FILE SIZE

The file you have created is shorter than 24 lines, the size of the screen. Therefore the entire file can be displayed on the screen. However, this is not typical. Usually, files have more than 24 lines and only a portion of the file can be visible at one time. In this case, you must learn to display any part of the file by moving the file on the screen. That way you can find the passage you want to change.

Before you learn how to locate passages in a file, increase the size of the file so it is larger than 24 lines.

1. Give the command

   EDLIN SAMPLE.TXT

   to begin the editing process.

2. Then type

   L

   to display the six lines of your file on the video screen. Notice that line 1 has an asterisk at the beginning, marking it as the current line. If you want to make a printed listing of this file, complete with the EDLIN line numbers, turn on your printer and type

   ^P

   Give the command

   L

   again. The EDLIN listing on the screen will also appear at your printer. If you leave the printer engaged during this session, you will have a printed record of everything you typed and also what EDLIN displayed for you.

3. Now give the copy command (C)

   1,6,7C

   to double the size of your file. As you can see, this command has three parameters that are separated by commas and placed in front of the command. The first two parameters (1 and 6) specify the range of lines to be copied. The third parameter (7) tells EDLIN where to place the copy of lines 1-6. After you give this command, your file has 12 lines. The current line will be 7.

4. Give the command

   L

to see all 12 lines. Notice the asterisk on line 7 indicating the current line. The result will look like Figure 4.1.

5. Give the copy command a second time but with different parameters to make the file 24 lines long:

    1,12,13C

6. To see what you have done, type

    L

7. To double your file a third time, type

    1,24,25C

Your file now has 48 lines.

DISPLAYING LINES WITH THE L COMMAND

You have already seen that the L command displays lines of the file on the video screen. The current line is in the middle of the screen and

Figure 4.1: *Doubling the file size with the COPY command*

```
C>EDLIN SAMPLE.TXT
End of input file
*1,6,7C
*L
        1: This is the first line of my file SAMPLE.TXT.
        2: This is the second line.
        3: This is the third line.
        4: This is the fourth line.
        5: This is the fifth line.
        6: This is the sixth line.
        7:*This is the first line of my file SAMPLE.TXT.
        8: This is the second line.
        9: This is the third line.
       10: This is the fourth line.
       11: This is the fifth line.
       12: This is the sixth line.
*_
```

adjacent lines are shown on either side. You can also use the L command with one or two parameters, to display a selected group of lines that are anywhere in your file regardless of the current line number. For example:

    1. Give the command

        1,6L

    You will see the first six lines of the file. Notice that there is no asterisk to mark the current line. Line 25 is current (from the C command) and that line does not show in this display.

    2. Give the command

        L

    without parameters to see that line 25 is still current. The L command does not change the current line number.

DISPLAYING LINES WITH THE P COMMAND

    You have been looking at the file with the L command. However, you can view the file more systematically with the P (for page) command. This command can display 23 lines of your file, just like the L command. However, unlike the L command, the current line is automatically moved to the last line in the display.

    If the P command is given without a parameter, the display begins with the line following the current line. To see how the P command works, do the following steps.

    1. Give the command

        1P

    The first 23 lines of your file will be displayed. The parameter tells EDLIN to start the display with line 1 regardless of the current line number. Notice, however, that 23, the last line in the display, is now the current line.

    2. Give the command

        P

but do not include a parameter this time. The next 23 lines, lines 24 to 46, are displayed and line 46, the last line in the display, is marked as the current line.

3. The current line number can be changed in several different ways. However, it is most convenient to move the current line with the P command and two identical parameters. For example, give the command

   16,16P

to make line 16 current and to display that line.

4. Give the command

   L

and 23 lines around the current line will be displayed (Figure 4.2). (If the L command is given without parameters, the current line will be in the middle of the display unless you are near the top or bottom.) The current line stays at 16 because the L command does not change it. You can also combine two EDLIN commands. That is, you can give the command

   16,16PL

This command combines the two previous commands (P and L). It moves the current line and displays 23 lines around the new current line.

SEARCHING FOR A PARTICULAR WORD

Since EDLIN can only display a maximum of 23 lines on the video screen at one time, you must learn how to view the part of your file that you want to change. With a small file, you can quickly move through the lines by displaying one page at a time with the P command. For example, you can give the command

   1P

to see the first page. Then repeatedly give the command

   P

without a parameter to move consecutively through the pages. However, with larger files, this can be time consuming. It is more convenient to let EDLIN find the location for you. You can locate a particular word with the S (for search) command. For example, to find the first occurrence of the word *line,* give the command

1Sline

The 1 before the S tells EDLIN to start its search at line 1. You will see:

1:   This is the first line of my file SAMPLE.TXT.

on the video screen because the word *line* appears on the first line.

There are a few peculiarities with the search command. First, you must be careful to match uppercase and lowercase letters. That is, you cannot find the word *line* if you search for *LINE* because the cases do not match.

A second problem can occur because the S command only searches in the forward direction. Thus, if no parameter is given, EDLIN searches for the next occurrence of the given word immediately after the current line. However, if you give EDLIN a specific line number with the search command, it makes that line current and begins the search there.

Figure 4.2: *Moving the current line number to 16*

```
16:*This is the fourth line.
 5: This is the fifth line.
 6: This is the sixth line.
 7: This is the first line of my file SAMPLE.TXT.
 8: This is the second line.
 9: This is the third line.
10: This is the fourth line.
11: This is the fifth line.
12: This is the sixth line.
13: This is the first line of my file SAMPLE.TXT.
14: This is the second line.
15: This is the third line.
16:*This is the fourth line.
17: This is the fifth line.
18: This is the sixth line.
19: This is the first line of my file SAMPLE.TXT.
20: This is the second line.
21: This is the third line.
22: This is the fourth line.
23: This is the fifth line.
24: This is the sixth line.
25: This is the first line of my file SAMPLE.TXT.
26: This is the second line.
27: This is the third line.
*_
```

If the word you want to find is located between the beginning of the file and the current line, the S command will not find it unless a parameter is given. Thus, even if line 1 is current, you cannot find a string in line 1 unless you give the number 1 as a parameter. This feature of the S command is an advantage when you want to find a word that appears several times. Then, you can repeat the same search command without a parameter to find the next occurrence. EDLIN moves down each time you repeat the command.

Let us look at another example of how the S command works.

1. Give the command

    Sline

    and line 2 of your file is displayed because it is the next occurrence of the word *line.*

2. Press F3 and Return to repeat the command. The following line will be displayed and then made current. If EDLIN cannot find the string specified in the S command, it displays the error message:

    Not found

    and the current line is not changed. If this happens, check to see if you misspelled the word or if the current line is already past the place you want to find.

EDLIN LINE NUMBERS

As you have seen, EDLIN assigns a line number to each line. The numbers run consecutively, starting with 1. Line numbers can be used to specify where a command is to start; two numbers can specify a range of lines. You also saw that you can make a particular line current by giving the line number twice with the P command.

The line numbers are associated with the text in memory (but as you have seen, the line numbers are not placed into the file). To obtain a listing of your file showing the EDLIN line numbers, engage the printer with

    ^P

Then type

    1,#L

This lists all lines of the file. With a printed listing it is easier to make changes to your file because you can readily identify the corresponding line numbers. However, remember that the numbers associated with each line may change if you insert or delete lines. When you delete a line from your file, the remaining lines are renumbered. To prevent the line numbers from changing, start editing from the bottom of the file and work upward. This way, all the numbers from the previous version will stay the same. Let us see how this works.

Suppose you have a printout of a 48-line file containing the EDLIN line numbers. You want to delete lines 10, 30, and 40. If you start at the top of the program, deleting line 10 first, then the line originally numbered 11 becomes 10 after the deletion. Line 12 becomes 11, line 30 becomes 29, line 40 becomes 39, and so on. If you delete the original line 30, which is now numbered 29, all remaining line numbers will be changed again. Thus, the third line to be deleted is now numbered 38 rather than the original 40.

By contrast, suppose you reverse the process, deleting from the bottom up. If you delete line 40 first, then all lines beyond 40 are renumbered, but not those before it. The original line 30 is still 30, and the original line 10 is still 10. When line 30 is deleted next, lines numbered less than this are not changed. You can confidently delete line 10 next, since its number has not changed. You should add new lines in the same way—from the bottom up.

HOW TO ALTER TEXT

In the previous sections you learned how to change the current line number, how to display portions of the edit buffer on the video screen and printer, and how to search for a string of characters. Although you inserted new lines between the original ones with the I command, you did not alter the existing lines. In the following sections you will learn how to insert and delete entire lines as well as individual words.

DELETING LINES

Remember that alterations are made relative to the current line number. The D command, given with no parameters, deletes the current line. However, it is safer to use one or two parameters with the D command to delete specific lines, as shown below:

1. Give the command

   23D

to delete line 23. (Remember, all the remaining lines in the file are renumbered.) The new line numbered 23 (which was originally line 24) becomes the current line. If you now want to delete a line beyond 23, do not use the original line numbers. Instead, you should inspect the region with the L or P command to find the new line number.

2. To delete a group of lines, give two parameters to the D command. For example, give the command

    23,29D

    and lines 23 through 29 are deleted. This command also makes the new line 23 the current line and it renumbers the previous line 30 to line 23, line 31 to line 24, and so forth.

INSERTING LINES

You previously added new lines with the I (for insert) command. You gave the I command without a parameter and then typed material for the new lines. The lines are placed before the current line. That is, if the first line is current, the new material is placed at the very beginning. You also gave the command:

    #I

to add lines to the end.
Now let's add lines to the middle.

1. Give the command

    21I

    to insert text between lines 20 and 21.

2. Now type the following line:

    Line inserted with the I command.

    The text will appear after line 20. The new line is numbered 21 and the original line 21 is renumbered 22. If you make a mistake while typing the new material, use the Backspace key to delete the incorrect character.

3. When you have completed typing the new material, press

^Break

to end the insert mode and return to command mode.

ADDING CONTROL CHARACTERS

Sometimes you need to add control characters to a text file. For example, ^H makes the printer back up so you can print a second character over the previous one. This is useful for creating certain symbols such as the Greek letter theta (a minus sign over a zero), the Greek letter phi (a fence symbol over a zero), and an interesting footnote character (a right parenthesis over a left parenthesis). You can make the computer beep at a specific point in your file by putting ^G at that spot. An application discussed in the next chapter needs the Esc character, which is ^[.

You cannot generally type control characters when you are in insert mode because EDLIN will interpret these control characters as commands. However, if you first type ^V, then you can press the corresponding letter key in *uppercase.* Do not use lowercase or a control key. For example, to enter ^H into EDLIN, type ^VH and to enter ^G, type ^VG. Similarly, Esc is given as ^V[.

REPLACING CHARACTERS

You have learned how to make changes to the text by deleting one or more lines or by inserting new lines. You also learned how to search for a word. But sometimes you want to change only one character or word. Then it is convenient to alter just these few characters in the existing line instead of deleting the entire line and retyping it. There are two ways to change only part of a line. The easiest way replaces one word with another, the harder way uses the DOS editing commands that you learned in Chapter 2. We will only consider the easier method.

You can replace one word with another by using the R (for replace) command. The command syntax is similar to the search command. Add a ^Z and the second word to the end of the first. For example, say you want to replace *second* with SECOND:

1. Give the command

1,3Rsecond ^ZSECOND

to locate the word *second,* that lies between lines 1 and 3, and replace it with SECOND. Notice that a ^Z character marks the end of the first word and the beginning of the second. Since the replacement command changes each occurrence between the given line numbers, you must be careful to restrict the range if you only want to make one change. You can confine the action to one line by making the first and second parameters the same.

2. To change the line

    9:   This is the third line.

    to

    9:   This is the ninth line.

    give the command

    9,9Rthird^Zninth

    As with the search command, the replace command begins with the line after the current line unless a starting line number is given. Then it begins with the line given as the first parameter. Furthermore, the replacement continues through the file until the line number given as the second parameter is reached. If a second parameter is not given, replacement continues to the end.

3. To change every occurrence of the word *This* to the word *That,* give the command

    1RThis^ZThat

    In this case, the replacement begins at line 1 and continues to the end because there is no second parameter to tell it when to stop.

4. If you want to view the changes, type the list command (L).

HOW TO MOVE A BLOCK OF TEXT

Sometimes it is necessary to move several lines of text from one place in the file to another. This is called a *block move.* You can move a block of text with the EDLIN M (for move) command. For example, to move the block of text containing lines 10 to 18 to the position in front of line 35, give the command:

10,18,35M

COMPLETING THE EDITING SESSION

After you have finished making your changes, give the E command. Then, EDLIN writes the new version to the new disk file, renames the extension of the original file to BAK, and gives the original name to the new version. It is a good idea to give this command every 10 to 15 minutes during an editing session. Let us see why.

If power fails or if the computer is accidentally turned off or unplugged during an editing session, the original file will be intact because it is located on a disk. However, you will lose the changes you made because they have not yet been saved on a disk. To avoid such a loss, you should frequently end the editing session with the E command and then restart EDLIN. (Press the F3 key to repeat the previous command line.) Then you cannot lose more than 10 or 15 minute's worth of work. But there is another way to end the editing session. Suppose you make a typing error that causes a drastic mistake. For example, if you accidentally type the command #D, all text from the current line to the end is deleted. If something like this happens, you can return to a previous version of your file with the Q (for quit) command. Then EDLIN returns to DOS and abandons the changes you made during the current editing session. The original file is unchanged and can be edited again. When you give the Q command, EDLIN requests verification.

SUMMARY

In this chapter, you have learned how to use the text editor EDLIN. This is a general-purpose editor that allows you to create and modify a text file with just a few commands.

You will need to use EDLIN if it is the only editor provided with your computer. Although the operation of EDLIN is less convenient than a specialized word processor, it is a convenient tool for correcting and modifying existing files and it does come free with DOS.

In learning about EDLIN's operation, you studied the edit buffer and the commands for manipulating text in the buffer. You also learned how to change the current line, locate strings of characters, and display and alter text in the edit buffer. A summary of the EDLIN commands is given in Chapter 10.

5 Organizing Your Hard Disk and Fine Tuning Your System

In this chapter you will write programs to set up your computer for the particular hardware that is present and to select the features you are interested in. You begin by setting up the hard disk in the next section. If you do not have a hard disk, skip over this part. Begin with the section called Establishing a Search Path. If your hard disk is already working, skip over to the section called Establishing a DOS Subdirectory.

HOW TO SET UP A HARD DISK

A new hard disk must be partitioned and formatted before it can be used. These two steps may have been done by the dealer before you purchased the computer. However, if you purchased it by mail order or directly from IBM, it may not have been prepared for use. If you're not sure, it does no harm to format your hard disk a second time if there are no programs on it. Give the command:

    DIR C:

If you see the message:

    Invalid drive specification

then your hard disk has not been prepared.

If your hard disk holds 20M bytes (that is, 20 million bytes, or megabytes) or more, be sure to have DOS version 3 (3.1, 3.2, or 3.3) or later. DOS version 2 (2.0 or 2.1) is very inefficient; it will waste a large part of your hard-disk space. Furthermore, DOS Version 3.0 has bugs.

PARTITIONING YOUR HARD DISK

There are several incompatible disk operating systems you can run on your computer. DOS allows you to partition your hard disk so that each different disk-operating system you want to use can work in a different part of the disk. If you only want to use DOS (MS-DOS or PC-DOS), you will devote the entire hard disk to DOS.

MS-DOS cannot handle disks larger than 32M bytes. Therefore, if your hard disk is larger than 32M bytes, DOS assigns the first 32M bytes to drive C. Then, if you have DOS Version 3.3, but not an earlier version, you can assign the remaining space to drive D.

You must use the FDISK program to partition your hard disk before it can be used. This program must be run even if you will only be using DOS, and your disk is smaller than 32M bytes.

1. If your computer is turned off, put the main DOS disk in drive A and turn on the computer. If the computer is already on, insert the system disk and press the Ctrl, Alt, and Del keys simultaneously.

2. Partition the hard disk by giving the command

    FDISK

and pressing the Return key. You will be presented with a menu like the one shown in Figure 5.1.

3. Type the number 4 and press the Return key to display the partition data. If near the bottom of the screen you see the line:

   No partitions defined

   it means that your hard disk has not been partitioned. If you don't see this line, your disk has already been partitioned and you should skip over to the section called Formatting Your Hard Disk. Otherwise, continue with the next instructions.

4. Press Esc to return to the main menu.

5. Type the number 1 and press the Return key to select the first item: Create DOS partition.

6. On the next screen, if you see the message:

   1. Create Primary DOS partition
   2. Create Extended DOS partition
   Enter choice: [1]

Figure 5.1: *The FDISK menu*

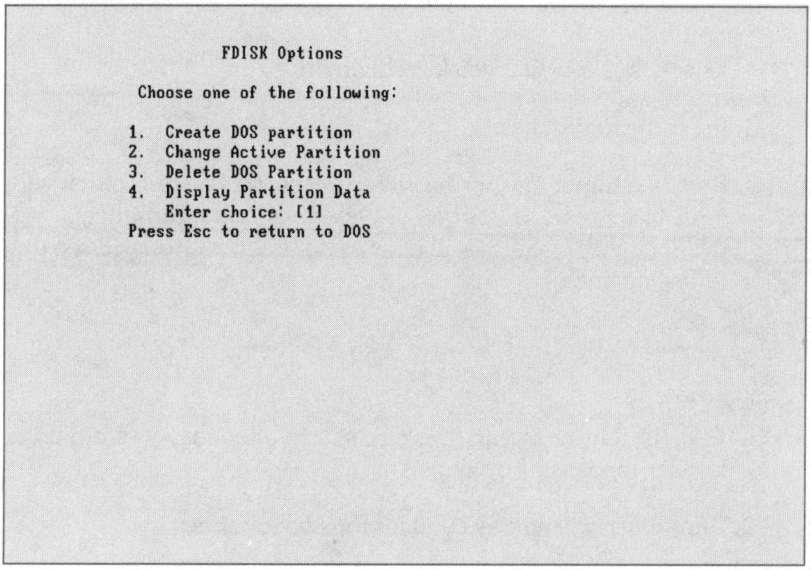

```
                    FDISK Options

         Choose one of the following:

         1.   Create DOS partition
         2.   Change Active Partition
         3.   Delete DOS Partition
         4.   Display Partition Data
              Enter choice: [1]
         Press Esc to return to DOS
```

it means that your hard disk is larger than 32M bytes. Then FDISK can create two logical disks, C and D, on your hard disk. Press Return to select the default of 1.

The next screen shows:

```
Do you wish to use the maximum size
for a DOS partition and make the DOS
partition active (Y/N).........? [Y]
```

Press Return.

Alternatively, if your DOS version is earlier than 3.3 or your hard disk is 32M bytes or smaller, you will see the line:

```
Create DOS Partition
Do you wish to use the entire fixed
disk for DOS [Y/N]................? [Y]
```

press the Return key to select the default of Y.

7. The following message appears:

```
System will now restart

Insert DOS diskette in drive A:
Press any key when ready...
```

Check that your DOS disk is still in drive A.

8. Press the Return key.

9. Because the computer has been reset, the system clock will have to be reset. If your DOS disk does not automatically set the date and time, you will have to do that now. You will see the following lines:

```
Current date is Tue 01-01-1980
Enter new date (mm-dd-yy):
```

Give the date as month (two digits), a hyphen, day (two digits), a hyphen, and year (two digits).

10. The screen will now ask you for the current time:

```
Current time is 10:03:25.34
```

Give the hours and minutes (two digits each), separated by a colon.(For Version 3, you can also use a period. Then you won't have to press the Shift key).

In the next step, we will format the portion of your hard disk that has been designated as drive C. If your hard disk is larger than 32M bytes, you can designate the remainder of the disk as drive D. We will consider this step at the end of this chapter.

FORMATTING YOUR HARD DISK

Now that your hard disk has been partitioned, it must be formatted. Be careful not to accidentally format your system disk in drive A. Run the format program as you did in Chapter 3. Be sure that the date and time are correctly set.

1. Give the command

   FORMAT C:/S/V

   You learned in Chapter 3 that the format program destroys all data on the disk. Therefore, you must be careful not to accidentally format a good disk, especially a hard disk that holds a large amount of information. Therefore, when you try to format a hard disk, newer versions of the format program give you a warning in case you meant to format a floppy disk, but gave the hard-disk letter by mistake.

2. When you see the message

   Warning, All Data on Non_removable
   Disk Drive C: Will be Lost!
   Proceed with Format (Y/N)?

   type

   Y

   and then press the Return key. The message

   Formatting...

   appears on the screen and the red light on the hard disk will be lighted. You can watch the cylinder numbers change on the screen as the formatting progresses. This should be the only time you have to format your hard disk. The process may take several minutes. The /S switch in the FORMAT command adds a copy of the DOS system to the hard disk. Then you will be able to start up your computer directly from the hard disk if there is no floppy disk in drive A.

3. When you give the /V switch, you will see the line

   Volume label (11 characters, ENTER for none)?

   Type something that identifies your computer such as your name, department name, or office number. Of course, a disk name is more useful for removable media like floppy disks that can easily be mixed up.

   After the formatting is finished and you have selected a volume name you will see a display like the one in Figure 5.2. The first number after the heading gives the total disk space, about 31M bytes here. The next number shows the space taken up by DOS and the third number is the number of unusable locations on the disk. The nearly 40K bytes of unusable space is not a

---

Figure 5.2: *Summary of disk and memory usage*

```
Volume PERSONNEL created Nov 12, 1986 5:33p

    31768576 bytes total disk space
       45056 bytes in 3 hidden files
       40960 bytes in bad sectors
    31712560 bytes available on disk

      655360 bytes total memory
      523136 bytes free
```

large amount for a disk of this size. However, be sure to record this number in a notebook for future reference. If a printer is attached, turn it on. Hold the shift key and press the PrtSc key to obtain a printout of this information on the screen.

It is a good idea to check the hard disk every day for the first few weeks with the command

    CHKDSK C:

This gives you a listing similar to the one above. Recheck the number of bad sectors in this list daily over the first few weeks to see if it is increasing. If the number does increase, it means you have a defective disk and you should return it to the supplier for another.

ESTABLISHING SUBDIRECTORIES

Now that the hard disk has been partitioned and formatted and it contains a copy of DOS, you can establish the subdirectories. If you skipped over the previous section because your hard disk was already working properly, this is where you begin again.

A hard disk can hold many files. Therefore you must establish a systematic way to locate the information you want. If there are several hundred files in the same directory, the listing of the file names gets very long. Furthermore, it is difficult to search through the file names because the listing is usually in a random order.

If you subdivide the hard disk into separate areas, you can keep related files together. There are several ways to organize a hard disk. However, we will select a simple but powerful way. We use the main area called the *root directory* only for a few essential programs. Then we establish auxiliary directories from the root directory. The auxiliary directories are called *subdirectories.*

Each subdirectory can contain files for a particular subject. The name of a subdirectory, like the name of a disk, consists of 1 to 11 characters, including uppercase letters, hyphens, underlines, and blanks. If you type the name in lowercase letters, they are converted to uppercase. You might have one subdirectory for each staff member in an office— one named JOHN, another named SUSAN, and so forth. Subdirectory names can also be chosen by subject; for example, REPORT for reports, MEMOS for memos, PURCHASE for purchase orders, and so on. There can be subdirectories named LOTUS, PASCAL, DBASE, and BASIC.

Before you create a subdirectory, check the newly formatted hard disk to see that everything is in order.

1. Give the command

   C:

   This makes the root directory of the hard disk the current one. This directory contains the three DOS files that were placed in the root directory by the formatting program. Two of these files are hidden because they are only used by your computer. The other file is named COMMAND.COM.

2. To make sure that this file is present, type the following command:

   DIR

You create a subdirectory with the built-in DOS command MD (Make Directory). Now, any directory you create with the MD command will be a subdirectory of the root directory because the root directory is current. It is possible to create a subdirectory of a subdirectory by making the subdirectory current and then giving the MD command from there. Of course it is also possible to create a subdirectory of a subdirectory of a subdirectory. However, you will generally find it easier to work with only a single level of subdirectories. That is, you should create all your subdirectories from the root directory, if possible.

When you give the MD command, the new directory becomes a subdirectory of the current directory. Therefore, if you want to have only one level of subdirectory, you must be certain that the root directory is current before giving the MD command. For example, if you give the commands

   MD JOHN
   MD SUSAN

when the root directory is current, both will be subdirectories of the root directory (see Figure 5.3). On the other hand, suppose that you give the MD command to create a subdirectory named SUSAN while the subdirectory named JOHN is current. Then the subdirectory SUSAN will be a subdirectory of JOHN (see Figure 5.4).

To ensure that the root directory is current, give the command

   CD\

Figure 5.3: *Two subdirectories of the root directory*

```
   Directory of   C:\

COMMAND   COM    23791  12-30-85   12:00p
JOHN             <DIR>  10-07-86    9:29p
SUSAN            <DIR>  10-07-86    9:29p
        3 File(s)     987424 bytes free
```

Figure 5.4: *A subdirectory of a subdirectory*

```
   Directory of   C:\JOHN

  .              <DIR>  10-07-86    9:29p
  ..             <DIR>  10-07-86    9:29p
SUSAN            <DIR>  10-07-86    9:29p
        3 File(s)     987424 bytes free
```

(for Change Directory). If drive C is not the current drive, type these two commands

```
C:
CD\
```

Notice that a backslash appears in these commands. You have seen that the forward slash designates a DOS switch. However, the backslash character is different; it means that a subdirectory name will follow. The special form

```
CD\
```

refers to the root directory. The prompt does not change when you give this command.

Creating a DOS Subdirectory

You will now establish a subdirectory to contain the programs found on the two original DOS disks. Then you will copy these programs from the floppy disks to the hard disk.

1. Give the command

   ```
   C:
   ```

   if C is not the current drive.

2. Give the command:

   ```
   CD\
   ```

   to ensure that the root directory is current. (The subdirectory name does not appear in the prompt.)

3. Create a new subdirectory by giving the command

   ```
   MD DOS
   ```

   Be sure to put a space between the command and its parameter. This command establishes a subdirectory named DOS.

4. Type

   ```
   DIR
   ```

and you will see the name

DOS <DIR>

in the directory listing. The <DIR> symbol means that this entry is a subdirectory and not a file name.

5. Now you need to make the new subdirectory current in order to work with it. Type the command

CD DOS

You can also give the command

CD\DOS

These two commands do the same thing this time. However, they have different meanings. The first command refers to a subdirectory of the current directory; the second command refers to a subdirectory of the root directory. If a subdirectory named JOHN were current and you gave the first command, DOS would try to find a subdirectory belonging to JOHN. The second command makes the root directory current first and then moves to the requested subdirectory.

6. The subdirectory named DOS is current. Make a listing to see what it contains by typing

DIR

You will see the following information on your screen:

Volume in drive C is PERSONNEL
Directory of C:\DOS

. <DIR> 11-12-85 5:35p
.. <DIR> 11-12-85 5:35p

You can see that this is a listing of subdirectory DOS on drive C that is named PERSONNEL. No files are shown. But there are two directory entries that do not seem to have names. One name consists of a single dot and the other a double dot. These two entries are part of every subdirectory listing (but not the root directory); they contain information DOS needs. The double dot identifies the parent directory, that is, the directory this subdirectory was created from. The single dot refers to the current directory.

7. If you now type

   DIR ..

you will see a directory listing of the parent directory (the root directory in this example). Because the single dot refers to the present directory, be careful not to give the command

   DEL .

accidentally, because you will delete all files from the current directory.

CHANGING THE DOS PROMPT

The regular DOS prompt gives the name of the current drive followed by the > symbol. It does not identify the current directory name. To find out the name of the current directory you have to type the CD command (without a parameter). Thus the command

   CD

will produce the line

   C:\

if the root directory is current, or the line

   C:\DOS

if the DOS subdirectory is current. However, it is much more convenient to tell DOS to identify the name of the current directory automatically as part of the prompt. To do so, follow these steps:

1. Make the root directory current with the command

   CD\

2. Then type

   PROMPT PG

   The prompt will change to:

   C:\>

   (The meanings of $P, $G, and other symbols are defined in Chapter 10 under the heading PROMPT.)

3. Change to the DOS subdirectory with the command

   CD DOS

   Now the prompt appears as

   C:\DOS>

   and you know right away that the DOS subdirectory is current. You can change the prompt back to the default by giving the command

   PROMPT

   without a parameter. But once you get used to seeing the subdirectory identified in the prompt, you won't want to change back.

COPYING DOS PROGRAMS TO THE NEW SUBDIRECTORY

When you have a hard disk, you can copy all your programs from floppy disks to the hard disk. Then you can put the floppies away and save them in case your hard disk crashes. To copy your programs onto your hard disk, do the following:

1. Put the main DOS disk in drive A.

2. Make the hard disk current with the command

   C:

3. Make the DOS subdirectory current with the command

   CD\DOS

4. Copy the DOS programs to the hard disk with the command

   COPY A:*.*

5. After all the files have been copied to the hard disk, change to the second DOS disk and repeat the command.

HOW TO ESTABLISH A SEARCH PATH

If you skipped over the previous sections because you did not have a hard disk, this is where you continue.

As you know, you can execute a program on the current disk simply by typing its name. On the other hand, if a program is located on another disk or subdirectory, you must type the drive name, subdirectory name, and the program name. For example, if EDLIN is on the current disk, you can create a new EDLIN file by typing

EDLIN NEWFILE

However, if EDLIN is on drive A but another drive is current, you must give the command

A:EDLIN NEWFILE

For a floppy-disk system, it is convenient to make drive B current and do your work there. Then the programs, such as EDLIN, are kept on drive A. However, with a hard disk, you should keep your programs in one subdirectory, say DOS, and make another subdirectory current for your work. Then you must establish a *search path* that tells DOS where to find your programs if they are not on the current directory. The built-in command PATH can direct DOS to your programs. For a floppy-disk system, give the command

PATH A:\

Then no matter what disk is current, DOS will look for your programs on drive A if it can't find them on the current directory. (Give the PATH command without a parameter to see if the path has already been defined.)

If you have a hard disk and have chosen the subdirectory DOS for your programs, give the command

PATH C:\DOS

Now, DOS will look for your programs in the subdirectory named DOS when they are not in the current directory. You can override the PATH command by specifying a different directory in your command if you want to do so.

HOW TO CREATE DOS CONFIGURATION FILES

Each time DOS is started, it looks for two disk files: CONFIG.SYS and AUTOEXEC.BAT. These files are not required for the operation of DOS and are not even supplied with DOS. However, if you create them yourself, you can use them to configure DOS for your particular requirements. If you do not provide these files, DOS will choose default values that may not be best for your system.

CREATING THE CONFIG.SYS FILE

Before you begin creating your CONFIG.SYS file, make sure it doesn't already exist on your system disk A or C. Some computers use these files to operate the peripherals.

1. Put your system disk in drive A.

2. Go to drive A with the command

    A:

3. Type the command

    DIR CONFIG.SYS

    and look for the message

    file not found

    This means that the CONFIG.SYS file does not exist. On the other hand, if you see a line like this

    CONFIG SYS 128 8-17-86 2:19p

the file does exist. Both the primary name and the extension must match. Of course, the file size (128 bytes here) and the creation date will be different. If you found the CONFIG.SYS file, skip over the next six steps. If you don't have CONFIG.SYS already, read ahead.

4. Go to the hard disk with the command

    C:

With a floppy system, give the command

    A:

5. If you have a hard disk, go to the root directory with the command

    CD\

6. If you have not established a search path with the PATH command as described in the previous section, please go back and do that now. You need to use your editor, and it should be in the subdirectory referenced by the PATH command.

7. Start the editor you use to create files. If it is WordStar, be sure to select the N (nondocument) mode rather than the D (document) mode. Otherwise DOS will not be able to read your file. (Alternatively, you can use the DOS COPY CON command. See Chapter 8 for details.)
    To use the DOS editor, give the command:

    EDLIN CONFIG.SYS

8. At the * prompt, type the EDLIN insert command

    I

and press the Return key.

9. If you have a 10 megabyte (MB) hard disk, type the following three lines:

    BUFFERS = 16
    FILES = 14
    DEVICE = C:\DOS\ANSI.SYS

If you have a 20 or 30 MB hard disk, type these lines:

```
BUFFERS = 20
FILES = 14
DEVICE = C:\DOS\ANSI.SYS
```

For a floppy-disk system type

```
BUFFERS = 4
FILES = 14
DEVICE = ANSI.SYS
DEVICE = VDISK.SYS 250
```

The BUFFERS command speeds up disk operations by increasing the number of memory buffers. These buffers hold copies of information previously read from disk. Each time DOS needs to read the disk, it checks the buffers first to see if the information is already present in memory. If so, the information can be read more rapidly from the buffer than from the disk.

The number of buffers should be much larger for a hard-disk system than for a floppy system. A larger number of buffers keeps more data in memory. However, there are two disadvantages to increasing the number of buffers beyond the given values. If you have too many buffers, you reduce the size of working memory so that you cannot run large programs. Furthermore, as the number of buffers increases, it takes a longer time to search them for the desired data. You can experiment with your system to determine the most favorable number of buffers. However, you should start with the values given above.

The FILES command sets the largest number of disk files that can be used at one time. The default value is eight. However, DOS uses three of these for the peripherals. Some commercial programs require more than the default value.

The command

```
DEVICE = VDISK.SYS 250
```

executes the program VDISK.SYS which creates a *virtual disk* or *RAM disk* in main memory that appears to be another disk. The example specifies a size of 250K bytes. The RAM disk is a useful addition to a floppy-disk system because it provides another disk for your system. Furthermore, it operates many times faster than a floppy disk. It is even faster than a hard disk.

Remember, however, that the RAM disk reduces your working memory. Therefore, you should only use the 250K size if you have a full 640K bytes of memory. If you have less memory, reduce the number at the end of the VDISK command accordingly. For example, if you have 512KB of memory, use the command

```
DEVICE = VDISK.SYS 125
```

The RAM disk becomes drive C for a floppy-disk system. If you establish a RAM disk with a hard-disk system, the RAM disk becomes drive D.

The VDISK.SYS program is found on the DOS disk for version 3. Of course, the VDISK program can also be used with a hard-disk system. However, it does not provide such a noticeable increase in speed since hard disks are so much faster than floppy disks.

CHANGING THE CONFIG.SYS FILE

If your computer was configured when you got it, you may already have a CONFIG.SYS file. If so:

1. Make yourself a printed listing of the file with the command

   ```
   COPY CONFIG.SYS PRN
   ```

2. If you do not have a printer, give the command

   ```
   TYPE CONFIG.SYS
   ```

   so you can look at the contents.

3. Check the CONFIG.SYS listing for the BUFFERS, FILES, and DEVICE commands. If they are not present, use your editor to add them. The order is not important. That is, you may place them either at the top of the file or at the bottom. If these commands are present and the values are smaller, use your editor to increase them to the values shown.

CREATING THE AUTOEXEC.BAT FILE

The second file that DOS automatically reads each time your computer is turned on or restarted is called AUTOEXEC.BAT. You can place a list of commands in this file and DOS will carry out the corresponding operation each time you start up or reset the computer. Check to see if you have one by following these steps:

1. Put your system disk in drive A.

2. Go to drive A with the command

    A:

3. Type the command

    DIR AUTOEXEC.BAT

    and look for the message

    file not found

    This means that the AUTOEXEC.BAT file does not exist. On the other hand, if you see a line like this

    AUTOEXEC BAT 512 10-01-86 2:26p

    the file does exist. The primary name and the extension must match. Of course, the file size (512 bytes here) and the creation date will be different.

If you didn't find the AUTOEXEC.BAT file, create one by following these steps:

1. If you have a hard disk, make it current with the command:

    C:

    With a floppy system, give the command:

    A:

2. Go to the root directory of your hard disk with the command:

    CD\

3. Start the editor you use to create files. For the DOS editor, give

the command:

    EDLIN AUTOEXEC.BAT

4. At the * prompt, type the EDLIN insert command:

    I

and press the Return key.

5. Type the following lines:

```
ECHO OFF
BREAK ON
VERIFY ON
PATH A:\       (if you have a floppy-disk system)
PATH C:\;A:\   (if you have a floppy-disk system with RAM
               disk)
or PATH C:\DOS (if you have a hard-disk system)
```

You can use either uppercase or lowercase letters.

Let us go through these commands.

ECHO OFF   The first command turns off the ECHO feature. It reduces the amount of information displayed on the screen as the other commands are carried out. However, this command itself is shown on the video screen. If you have DOS Version 3.3, use the form

    @ECHO OFF

instead. The @ symbol will prevent this command from appearing on the screen.

BREAK ON   You may want to prematurely interrupt an executing program because you made a typing error in the command line. Holding the Ctrl key and pressing the Break key will stop a program only when there is keyboard input or video-screen output. But there may not be input or output during the beginning of a program. If the BREAK feature is turned on, DOS will check for ^Break more frequently. Because the default setting is off, you should turn it on in the AUTOEXEC file.

VERIFY ON   Normally when DOS writes to a disk file, it does not check to see if the information is correctly written. The third command turns on the verification feature so that DOS will check that each file is correctly written. Of course, when VERIFY is on, it takes longer to write a disk file. However, it is better to be safe even though it does take a little longer.

PATH . . .   The fourth line establishes a search path. You gave this command earlier from the keyboard. This command tells DOS where to look for a program when it cannot be found on the current disk. Use drive A for a floppy-disk system and drive C for a hard-disk system or a RAM disk. When this command is in the AUTOEXEC.BAT file, you will not have to type it from the keyboard.

Later you will want to add commands to the AUTOEXEC.BAT file to copy your editor, spreadsheet, and related programs to the RAM disk if you have established one.

If your editor program uses auxiliary files, as WordStar does, it will run faster if you put the auxiliary files in the RAM disk. Then you can configure WordStar to look for the auxiliary files on the RAM disk (C or D). To copy WordStar and its auxiliary programs from disk A to RAM disk C, put this command in the AUTOEXEC.BAT file:

```
COPY A:WS*.* C: >NUL
```

(The >NUL command reduces the amount of information displayed on the screen during the copy operation.)

HOW TO FIND THE COMMAND PROCESSOR

Earlier in this chapter you saw that DOS reads the system file COMMAND.COM from disk each time you turn on or reset the computer. When DOS is started from the hard disk, it knows that this file can be found on the hard disk. For a floppy system, DOS expects to find COMMAND.COM on drive A. But sometimes it is convenient to replace the system disk with another. Then you must place a copy of COMMAND.COM on this disk or tell DOS to find it on another disk. Let us see how to use the RAM disk to solve this problem.

If you have a floppy-disk system that uses DOS version 3 (3.1, 3.2, or 3.3) and you establish a RAM disk that has at least 25K bytes of space, add these two lines to your AUTOEXEC.BAT file:

```
COPY   A:COMMAND.COM   C:  >NUL
SET   COMSPEC = C:\COMMAND.COM
```

The first of these two commands copies the command processor from drive A to RAM disk C. The second command tells DOS to look for the command processor on drive C. After these two commands have been given, you never need a DOS disk in drive A after DOS has started up. If you want to see where DOS expects to find the command processor, give the command

```
SET
```

and DOS will respond with several lines of text. One line will look something like this:

```
COMSPEC = C:\COMMAND.COM
```

The symbol C:\ means that DOS will look for COMMAND.COM on drive C. This technique will not work with DOS version 2.

CREATING ADDITIONAL
DRIVES ON YOUR HARD DISK

In this section you will establish the remaining hard disk space above 32M bytes. If your hard disk is 32M bytes or smaller, skip over this section. You must have DOS Version 3.3 for this step.

Now that your hard disk has been partitioned, formatted, and divided into subdirectories, your computer is ready to go. However, if your hard disk is larger than 32M bytes, a portion of your hard disk is not usable yet. You might think that a 32M byte disk is very large. However if you have many programs and large amounts of data, you can easily fill this space. Therefore, you may need to use the remaining space on your hard disk.

Before establishing the remainder of a hard disk as drive D, ensure that you do not have a RAM disk D. If so, remove the VDISK command from your CONFIG.SYS file.

To prepare the remainder of your hard disk:

1. Start the partitioning program by giving the command

```
FDISK
```

and pressing the Return key. You will be presented with a menu like the one shown in Figure 5.1.

2. Select the default of 1 by pressing the Return key to select the first item: Create DOS partition.

3. On the next screen, you see the message

```
1. Create Primary DOS partition
2. Create Extended DOS partition
Enter choice: [1]
```

Type the number 2 and press Return. The next screen shows something like:

```
Create Extended DOS Partition
Current Fixed Disk Drive: 1

Partition Status    Type  Start  End  Size
C: 1        A  PRI DOS     0    770  771

Total disk space is 979 cylinders.
Maximum space available for partition
is 208 cylinders.

Enter partition size..........: [208]
```

4. Press Return to select the remaining space for D. The next screen shows

```
Partition Status    Type  Start  End  Size
C: 1        A  PRI DOS     0    770  771
    2           EXT DOS   771   978  208

Extended DOS partition created
```

5. Press Esc and you see

```
No logical drives defined

Total partition size is 208 cylinders
Maximum space available for logical
drive is 208 cylinders.

Enter logical drive size..........: [208]
```

6. Press Return to select the default size for drive D. The next screen shows

       Drv Start End Size
       D: 771   978 208

7. Press Esc and you return to the main menu.

8. Press Esc again and the following message appears

       System will now restart
       Insert DOS diskette in drive A:
       Press any key when ready...

    However, because drive C has been established, you can safely boot from it.

9. Remove any floppy disks and press Return. Your computer will boot from drive C in the usual way.

10. Give the command:

       FORMAT D:/V

    and the following message appears

       WARNING, ALL DATA ON NON-REMOVABLE DISK
       DRIVE D: WILL BE LOST!
       Proceed with Format (Y/N)?

11. Type

       Y

    and then press the Return key. The message

       Formatting...

12. Give a name to drive D and press Return. Record the number of bad sectors, if any, and check the value over the next few weeks using CHKDSK.

    Now your hard disk has both drives C and D. Of course, if your hard disk is larger than 64K bytes, you can partition it into additional parts.

SUMMARY

In this chapter, you have learned how to set up your computer so it will be easy to use. You saw how to partition and then format a hard disk, and how to establish subdirectories for more orderly operation. You learned how to increase the default number of disk buffers and number of files. Then you learned how to activate the BREAK command so you can stop a program prematurely and the VERIFY command to ensure that disk files are properly written. The PATH command tells DOS where to find your programs. You learned how to establish a RAM disk and a printer buffer to speed up the operation of your computer. You created the CONFIG.SYS and AUTOEXEC.BAT files that tell DOS to do things your way. This included setting up a RAM disk and getting DOS to read the command processor from the RAM disk. Finally, you split a large hard disk into two parts—32M bytes for drive C and the remainder for drive D. In the next chapter, you will learn how to use additional DOS commands.

6 Useful DOS Built-In Commands

In this chapter you will study DOS in detail, and learn to use the built-in commands TYPE, DIR, REN, DEL, and ERASE. At this point it is not necessary to learn all the details of these commands. However, you should frequently review the information in this chapter and the next one until you can use these commands with ease. After reading this chapter and Chapter 7, even an infrequent user of DOS should understand how to:

- Use the control characters ^C, ^S, ^P, Backspace, Esc, and ^Break
- Inspect the disk directory with DIR
- View a disk file with TYPE
- Change file names with REN
- Delete a file with DEL
- Change the current drive and directory

You should refer to this chapter frequently until you are comfortable with the above DOS operations.

BUILT-IN COMMANDS VERSUS DOS PROGRAMS

When DOS displays the system prompt, you can type a command and press the Return key. However, you must distinguish between two types of DOS commands. One type is built into DOS, that is, the instructions for the command are always in memory, ready to be carried out. The other type, which is called an external program, or simply a program, is stored as a file on disk.

Whenever your computer is running, a working copy of DOS is present in memory. The built-in commands are a part of DOS and so they too are present in memory. The built-in commands execute rapidly because they do not have to be copied from a disk before they can be run.

Since memory space is limited, the number of DOS built-in commands is limited to the following: BREAK, CD, CLS, COPY, DATE, DEL, DIR, MD, PATH, PROMPT, RENAME, RD, SET, TIME, TYPE, VER, VERIFY, and VOL. All the other DOS operations are performed by external programs.

You have already been introduced to some of the built-in commands. The information in this chapter will deal with the most important of these commands: TYPE, DIR, RENAME, DEL, and ERASE. You can find a discussion of all the built-in commands in Chapter 10.

HOW TO DISPLAY A FILE
WITH THE TYPE COMMAND

In Chapter 3 you learned that TYPE can be used to display a text file on the video screen. You also learned to distinguish between text files, which can be viewed with TYPE, and program files, which cannot. Let us look at this distinction in more detail.

Text files are coded in ASCII (American Standard Code for Information Interchange). Because they are in this form, they can be transmitted directly to an ASCII device like the video screen and you will be able to read them. By contrast, binary files, such as those with the file extension COM and EXE, would look like gibberish to you if you displayed them directly on the video screen using the TYPE command. They must first be translated to ASCII.

To view a text file on the video screen with TYPE, use the following command:

    TYPE d:*fname.ext*

d is the drive name and *fname.ext* is the ASCII file name. Of course, you may omit the drive name if the file is located on the current drive. You must give the complete file name, including the extension if there is one, and you cannot use the wild-card characters (? and ∗). You used TYPE previously when you gave the command

    TYPE SAMPLE.TXT

to examine the text file you made.

If your file is longer than one screen length, the TYPE command displays screen after screen of the file so rapidly that it is difficult to read. Therefore, you will want to stop or *freeze* the moving screen with the ^S or ^NumLock command. When you are ready to resume scrolling, press any key. You might find it convenient to alternately press ^S to freeze and resume scrolling.

As you saw in Chapter 3, you can send a disk file to the printer with the redirection symbol:

    TYPE DIREXE >PRN

If you do not have a printer, you can try out this command by redirecting to nothing:

    TYPE DIREXE >NUL

If you want to try out a command, but are not interested in the output from it, you can send it to the NUL device. DOS then simply discards the output and there is no indication of what has happened.

Another way to send a file to the printer (discussed in Chapter 3) is to engage the printer with ^P and give the regular TYPE command. Your file will then be printed.

HOW TO VIEW THE DIRECTORY WITH DIR

You have used the DIR command several times in the book so far. Let's now study this command in more detail. The DIR command can display the name of a single file, a group of files, or all files in the disk directory.

When you give the DIR command with a file-name parameter such as

    DIR SAMPLE.TXT

the requested file name is displayed on the video screen if DOS finds it in the directory. In addition, DOS also displays the file size and the date and time of creation. The listing might look like this:

    SAMPLE TXT 256 9-01-86 9:20p

However, if the file is not present in the directory, the error message

    File not found

is displayed. Thus you can use DIR to determine if a particular file is located on the disk.

    If you are not sure how the file name is spelled, you can use the DIR command with the wild-card symbols ? and *. For example, suppose that the file you want is an executable program and the file name begins with the letter C. Then you can give the commands

    DIR C*.COM

and

    DIR C*.EXE

to get a list of all the programs whose names begin with the letter C. To find the names of all programs on the disk, type

    DIR *.COM

and

    DIR *.EXE

    Remember from Chapter 3 that the command

    DIR SORT?

matches not only files named SORT1 and SORT2, but also SORT. That is, a blank in the file name also matches the question mark. Thus the commands

    DIR

and

    DIR *

give the same result as the command

        DIR *.*

because they list all file names in the directory. If you want to list only those file names that do not have file-name extensions, you must use the form:

        DIR *.

Hidden files do not show in the directory listing. When you formatted a system disk and then later ran the CHKDSK program, you saw that two hidden files were present. These are two files that are only used by the computer when it is first turned on. Since you have no use for them, they are hidden so they cannot be accidently erased. Sometimes disks that contain commercial programs have hidden files. In the next chapter you will see how to display the names of hidden files using CHKDSK.

USING SWITCHES WITH DIR

When a disk contains many files, the regular directory listing will not fit on one video screen. Rather, it scrolls off the top of the screen and you can only see one part of the listing at a time. You found this to be the case for the DOS disk in Chapter 3. It is possible, however, to tell DOS to rearrange the screen so you can see the whole directory at once. You can do so by using a switch.

As you already know, a slash character followed by a letter or other symbol is called a switch. The switch changes the operation of a command in some way. You used /S and /V switches to give additional information to the FORMAT command. In this example, you use the /W switch to specify a wide display and the /P switch to freeze the screen at the end of each page.

When you include the /W switch with the DIR command, you get a condensed but wide listing. The size, date, and time are omitted from the display so five file names can be placed on each line. Then the listing may fit on one screen. To see the results, give the command:

        DIR/W

As with the FORMAT switches, it is not necessary to put a space in front of the slash. The first few lines of the wide display might look like Figure 6.1. This display has ten columns of words on each line. But, because

each file name has two parts—the primary name and the extension—
there are just five file names on each line.

Another way to view large directories is to tell DOS to stop scrolling when the screen becomes full. You do this by including the /P (for
page) switch. The command is:

    DIR/P

When you are finished looking at the first screen, you can press any key to
go on to the next one. Your screen should look something like Figure 6.2.

When you use a file-name parameter with DIR, place the switch after
the file name. (Be careful to place a space before the file-name parameter
as usual.)

HOW TO CHANGE A FILE NAME WITH RENAME

You have seen that each file name in the directory corresponds to
a file stored on the disk. The directory entry contains the two parts of the
file name and other information such as the size, date, and time of creation, and a number or *pointer* that shows the location of the first part of
the file. You have also seen that a file name should be carefully chosen to
reflect the purpose of the file. However, you may want to change a file
name to one that is more meaningful. Or perhaps you want to save a
previous version of a file with a different name before copying a newer
version to that disk. For these reasons, the RENAME command is built
into DOS. This command does not alter a file in any way; it only changes
the name that is recorded in the disk directory.

The format of the RENAME command is

    RENAME OLD_NAME NEW_NAME

OLD_NAME, the first parameter, is the original file name and NEW_-
NAME, the second parameter, is the new file name. This command can
be abbreviated to

    REN OLD_NAME NEW_NAME

Since no drive names were given with the above parameters, the current
drive is used. You may, of course, rename a file on another disk. Then
you include the drive name for the first parameter. For example, the
command

    REN B:OLD_NAME NEW_NAME

Figure 6.1:　*A wide listing from the DIR command*

```
    Volume in drive A has no label
    Directory of  A:\

ANSI     SYS   ASSIGN   COM   ATTRIB   EXE   BACKUP   COM   BASIC    COM
BASICA   COM   CHKDSK   COM   COMMAND  COM   COMP     COM   DISKCOMP COM
DISKCOPY COM   EDLIN    COM   FDISK    COM   FIND     EXE   FORMAT   COM
```

Figure 6.2:　*First page of the DIR listing*

```
ANSI     SYS    1651   12-30-85   12:00p
ASSIGN   COM    1536   12-30-85   12:00p
ATTRIB   EXE    8247   12-30-85   12:00p
BACKUP   COM    6234   12-30-85   12:00p
BASIC    COM   19298   12-30-85   12:00p
BASICA   COM   36396   12-30-85   12:00p
CHKDSK   COM    9832   12-30-85   12:00p
COMMAND  COM   23791   12-30-85   12:00p
COMP     COM    4184   12-30-85   12:00p
DISKCOMP COM    5792   12-30-85   12:00p
DISKCOPY COM    6224   12-30-85   12:00p
DRIVER   SYS    1115   12-30-85   12:00p
EDLIN    COM    7508   12-30-85   12:00p
FDISK    COM    8173   12-30-85   12:00p
FIND     EXE    6416   12-30-85   12:00p
FORMAT   COM   11135   12-30-85   12:00p
GRAFTABL COM    1169   12-30-85   12:00p
GRAPHICS COM    3220   12-30-85   12:00p
JOIN     EXE    8955   12-30-85   12:00p
KEYBFR   COM    3291   12-30-85   12:00p
KEYBGR   COM    3274   12-30-85   12:00p
KEYBIT   COM    3060   12-30-85   12:00p
KEYBSP   COM    3187   12-30-85   12:00p
Strike a key when ready . . .
```

renames the file OLD_NAME on drive B.

If DOS cannot find the original file name, you will see the following error message:

    Duplicate file name or file not found

Only the second part of the error message applies at this time. Perhaps you have the wrong disk or you misspelled the file name.

Two different files on the same disk cannot both have the same name. If you try to change the name of a file to the name of an existing file, you get the same error message:

    Duplicate file name or file not found

This time, the first half of the message applies. In either case, check your spelling and use the DIR command to find out what the problem is.

USING WILD CARDS WITH RENAME

You can use the ? and * wild-card symbols to rename a group of files but these symbols must be used with care. The wild-card symbols can be safely used in identical positions in both file names to change a group of files. For example, the command

    REN *.TXT *.BAK

changes all TXT files to BAK files. You can also use a wild-card to save typing when you change a single file name. For example, the command

    REN LONGNAME.TXT *.BAK

renames the file LONGNAME.TXT to LONGNAME.BAK.

HOW TO DELETE A FILE WITH DEL AND ERASE

Because the storage space on a disk is limited, all of it may eventually be occupied by files. Therefore, it is sometimes necessary to delete files you no longer need. The built-in command ERASE and its shorter form DEL can delete a single file or a group of files. Both commands do exactly the same thing and work the same way. You can use whichever command you prefer. The format is

        ERASE FNAME

or

        DEL FNAME

Of course, the file name must include a disk drive if the file is not on the current drive. You can use wild-card symbols (carefully) in the file name. For example, the command

        DEL FNAME.TXT

deletes the single file named FNAME.TXT on the current drive. The command

        DEL FNAME.*

deletes all files with the primary name FNAME—for example, FNAME.TXT, FNAME.BAK, and FNAME.BK2. If DOS cannot find a file to match the parameter, even when wild-card symbols are used, it displays the following error message:

        File not found

        Be careful when you use ERASE or DEL because a mistake can cause serious problems. For example, you can delete all backup files on a disk by giving the command:

        DEL *.BAK

However, if you inadvertently type

        DEL *.BAS

by mistake, DOS will delete all BASIC files rather than all backup files.
        Whenever wild-card symbols are included in the file name, there is a potential for disaster, since several files can be deleted at one time. Therefore, when you give the command

        DEL * *

DOS requests verification by asking:

Are you sure (Y/N)?

You must answer Y if you want DOS to continue. Otherwise, the operation is terminated without further action.

You can add an extra measure of safety when deleting a group of files by using the DIR command first. For example, to erase all BAK files:

1. Give the command

   DIR *.BAK

   You will see a listing of all the BAK files in your directory.

2. Carefully examine the directory listing to ensure that the files listed there are the ones you want to delete.

3. Type the letters

   DEL

4. Press F3 to display the rest of the previous command. The line should look like this:

   DEL *.BAK

5. Press Return to delete the listing on your screen.

SUMMARY

In this chapter you learned about the built-in commands TYPE, DIR, REN, DEL, and ERASE. In the next chapter, you will learn about external DOS programs.

7 *Useful DOS Programs*

We have seen that several useful routines, called commands, are built into DOS. They can be readily executed because they are always present in memory. Additional routines that are less frequently used are found on the DOS disk. These routines are known as external programs. You already know how to display the names of the external programs by giving the DIR command and you know that these programs have the extension COM or EXE. We have already discussed four of these programs—CHKDSK, FORMAT, DISKCOPY, and SORT.

You also learned that an external program is executed simply by typing the first part of the file name, for example:

DISKCOPY

You must not type the COM or EXE extension. If the program you want to run is not available on the current drive, its location must be described by a PATH command given previously, or the drive name, followed by a colon preceding the file name. Thus, you must give the command

A:DISKCOPY

if the program is on drive A and that drive is not current. If you have not established a file search path with the PATH command, please go to Chapter 5 and do that now.

While there are many programs on both the main and the supplemental DOS disks, you will find that you use only a few of them regularly. In this chapter you learn about the most useful DOS programs—ATTRIB, COMP, FIND, LABEL, MORE, and ASSIGN. You also write two batch files to help locate a file on a hard disk.

HOW TO PROTECT A FILE
FROM ACCIDENTAL DELETION

You learned previously that a file can be marked as hidden so the file name does not show in the directory listing. It is also possible to mark a file as *read-only* with the ATTRIB program. Then the file cannot be deleted even though the name appears in the directory listing. Let us see when to use this feature.

When you write text files, such as letters and reports, you will probably want to change them from time to time. Therefore, you should not mark these files as read only because you will not be able to change them. On the other hand, there is no reason for you to change the external DOS programs such as CHKDSK and FORMAT. These programs are not marked as read only by DOS automatically, but it is a good idea to do so yourself so they cannot be accidentally erased. When these programs are *write protected* (marked as read-only), they can still be executed in the usual way and they can still be copied to another disk.

The DOS program ATTRIB can report the current state of the read-only attribute, it can set a file to read only, and it can remove read-only protection from a file. Let us see how it is used.

You can check the current state of the read-only attribute for the file SORT.EXE by giving the command:

ATTRIB SORT.EXE

You can also check a group of files by using wild cards in the file-name parameter. Thus,

ATTRIB *.COM

reports on all files with the extension COM. As usual, be sure to include a space between the command and its parameter.

If the file name given in the parameter is marked as read only, the ATTRIB program will respond with the following:

R   A:\SORT.EXE

If the file-name parameter contains wild cards, all matching files will be shown. The letter R at the beginning of the line designates a file as read only. On the other hand, if the read-only attribute is turned off or not set, the response will not include an R at the beginning of the line and will simply say

A:\SORT.EXE

If you want to change the read-only attribute, place the R parameter (with either a plus or minus sign) between the command and the filename parameter. For example, to turn on, or set the read-only attribute for a file named SORT.EXE, give the command:

```
ATTRIB  +R  SORT.EXE
```

To set all COM files to read-only status, give the command:

```
ATTRIB  +R  *.COM
```

Be sure to include two spaces, one in front of each parameter.

The R parameter is like a switch. However, the switches you used previously, for example /P or /W, begin with a slash. With those switches, there is only one option to choose and it lasts only for the duration of the current program. The read-only parameter, however, is not temporal; it continues in its current state until you change it. Therefore, since this switch has two states—on or off—it must have two forms. The +R parameter turns on the read-only attribute and the −R parameter turns it off. Of course, if the ATTRIB program is not on the current disk, you must include the drive name in the command.

If you try to erase the file that has the read-only attribute set, DOS will not carry out your command. Rather, it will display the error message:

```
Access denied.
```

You can remove the read-only attribute with the command:

```
ATTRIB  −R  SORT.EXE
```

The −R parameter turns off the feature.

Another file attribute, called the *archive* attribute, helps you make backup copies of your files. You learned earlier that it is important to make frequent backup copies of important disk files. If you have a hard disk, with 10MB of files, you need 30 floppy disks to make backup copies. Of course, it is not necessary to back up all files each time. Rather, it is only necessary to back up those files that have been changed since the previous time you made backup copies. Unfortunately, the DOS COPY command cannot determine whether a backup copy has already been made and copies all files each time you make backup copies. Because the archive attribute is automatically set when a file is created or altered, this attribute can be checked by a program designed for backing up

your files. Starting with DOS version 3.2, the XCOPY program is provided for this purpose. This program is discussed in Chapter 10.

The ATTRIB program can display the current state of the archive
attribute and it can also change the state. It is similar to the read-only
feature. The command

```
ATTRIB  – A  *.BAK
```

resets the archive attribute for all BAK files so they will not be backed
up. The command:

```
ATTRIB  *.*
```

lists each file on the disk and gives an A if the archive attribute is set and
an R if the read-only attribute is set.

You can change both attributes at once, but you must put spaces
on both sides of each switch. For example

```
ATTRIB  +R  +A  *.COM
```

HOW TO COMPARE TWO FILES WITH COMP

If you find two files with the same name on different disks, you
might wonder whether or not they are the same. Alternatively, if you
make a backup copy of a file, you might want to be sure that the copy
was correctly made. The first thing to check is the file size given in the
third column of the DIR command. If the sizes are different, the files cannot be identical. However, if the file sizes are the same, you can compare
the contents, byte by byte, with the COMP program.

To compare FILE1 on disk A to FILE2 on disk B, give the following
command:

```
COMP  A:FILE1  B:FILE2
```

The second file name can be omitted if it is the same as the first and is
located on the current disk. Wild cards can be used in the parameters to
compare groups of files. Thus, the command

```
COMP  *.TXT  *.BAK
```

compares all files with the extension TXT to all files with the same primary name but with the extension BAK. If only the drive names are

given, all files on one disk are compared to files of the same name on the other disk.

If two file are the same, the message

    Files compare OK

appears. However, if a mismatch is found, the location is given and the contents of the corresponding locations are given. If the two files are not the same size, the following message appears:

    Files are different sizes

You learned previously that text files have a ⌃Z to mark the end of the file. However, sometimes the end-of-file (EOF) marker is missing. (This is always the case for files created by redirection.) The missing EOF mark can cause trouble with certain programs that require the EOF marker. However, most programs do not need the EOF mark. If the EOF marker is missing, the COMP program reports:

    EOF mark not found

When COMP has completed its task, it gives the message

    Compare more files (Y/N)?

Type N if you are finished or Y to compare additional files.

HOW TO LOCATE TEXT WITH FIND

In Chapter 3 you learned to use the DOS program SORT, a filter that can arrange lines of text in alphabetical order. FIND is also a filter, and as you might guess from the name, locates a word or textual passage in a file. Because FIND is a filter, it is used in the same way as SORT, that is, it can be used with the fences and redirection you learned about in Chapter 3.

Let's try out a simple application:

1. If you have a hard disk, go to the root directory. If you have a floppy system, put the system disk in A and make it current.

2. Give the command

    DIR SAMPLE.TXT

to see if the file you made in Chapter 4 is there. If not, find where it is or go back to Chapter 4 and make a copy.

3. Give the command

   FIND "second" SAMPLE.TXT

   This tells FIND to search SAMPLE.TXT, the second parameter, and to display each line that contains the first parameter, *second.* The result will look like Figure 7.1.

4. Repeat the previous line but include the /N switch as the first parameter:

   FIND /N "second" SAMPLE.TXT

   This time, the corresponding line numbers are given in brackets as shown in Figure 7.2.

5. Repeat the command, but give the /V switch to reverse the sense of the command

   FIND /V "second" SAMPLE.TXT

   Now, each line that does *not* contain the word *second* is displayed.

6. The /C switch displays the number of lines that contain the word you are searching for. Give the command

   FIND /C "second" SAMPLE.TXT

   and you will see

   − − − − − SAMPLE.TXT:8

   because eight lines of the file contain the word *second.*

You can tell DOS to look through more than one file. For example, the command

   FIND /N "keyboard" FILE1 FILE2 FILE3

will search all three files. Each file is individually identified, so you can determine the location of the word *keyboard.*

Figure 7.1: *Display from the FIND program*

```
C:\>FIND "second" SAMPLE.TXT

---------- SAMPLE.TXT
This is the second line.
This is the second line.
This is the second line.
This is the second line.
This is the second line.
This is the second line.
This is the second line.
This is the second line.
```

Figure 7.2: *Line numbers identified with the /N switch*

```
D:\>FIND /N "second" SAMPLE.TXT

---------- SAMPLE.TXT
[2]This is the second line.
[8]This is the second line.
[14]This is the second line.
[20]This is the second line.
[26]This is the second line.
[32]This is the second line.
[38]This is the second line.
[44]This is the second line.
```

Two commands can be combined with a fence to search the output destined for the video screen. For example, consider the following line:

```
DIR | FIND "SYS"
```

As you know, the DIR command creates a directory listing that usually is displayed on the video screen. However, the fence directs the output to the FIND command instead. The parameter, "SYS", tells FIND to display all lines of the directory listing that contain the letters SYS.

Wild cards cannot be used for the file-name parameter of FIND. Furthermore, the quoted expression is case sensitive. That is, if you give the word "second" to the FIND command, it will not locate the word "Second" because of the capital S. To avoid this problem, you can search for the fragment "econd" instead.

HOW TO LOCATE AND SORT FILES ON A HARD DISK

After you have used a hard disk for a while, you will have many subdirectories and many more files. The time will come when you want to locate a disk file that you know is somewhere on the hard disk. The problem is that you cannot remember the subdirectory where the file is located. In this case, you can use the DOS FIND command to help you locate a file on the hard disk.

SELECTING SUBDIRECTORIES WITH FIND

If you have not created subdirectories of subdirectories, but instead have defined all subdirectories from the root directory, you can get a listing of the subdirectories with the command

```
DIR *
```

(Make sure drive C is current first.) This command will not only show the names of subdirectories, but it will also list file names that do not have extensions. Of course, file names with extensions will not be shown. We can filter out the file names and leave only the subdirectory names by using FIND to search for the symbol <DIR> because all subdirectories have <DIR> in the listing.

Give the command

```
DIR *. | FIND "<DIR>"
```

Be sure to include spaces after DIR and FIND, and type <DIR> in upper-case. As you can see, this command line contains two separate commands, DIR, and FIND, separated by a fence. This example tells DOS to send the output from the DIR command to the FIND program. The FIND program searches through the directory listing and selects those lines that contain the characters <DIR>, as all subdirectories do. Then only those lines are sent to the video screen. The listing on the screen will contain only subdirectories and will look somewhat like Figure 7.3 (depending on what subdirectories are on your particular hard disk).

ORDERING THE LIST WITH SORT

When DOS displays a listing of your subdirectory names, it generally lists them in chronological order. However, it is more useful to have the listing arranged in alphabetical order. We can order the listing with the SORT filter. Give the command:

DIR *. ¦ FIND "<DIR>" ¦ SORT

(You can use the F3 key to save some typing.) In this example there are three separate commands on one line, DIR, FIND, and SORT, and they

---

Figure 7.3: *DIR listing of subdirectories*

```
DOS          <DIR>     4-38-86     5:59p
EDIT         <DIR>     4-38-86     7:03p
FORTRAN      <DIR>     4-38-86     8:03p
BASIC        <DIR>     4-38-86     8:03p
LETTERS      <DIR>     4-38-86     8:18p
TK           <DIR>     4-38-86     8:53p
INSTALL      <DIR>     4-38-86     8:56p
PASCAL       <DIR>     4-38-86     9:04p
LOTUS        <DIR>     4-38-86     9:08p
PROGRAMS     <DIR>     5-01-86    10:28a
REPORTS      <DIR>     5-05-86     8:44p
SIDEWAYS     <DIR>     5-06-86     6:45p
TOPVIEW      <DIR>     5-06-86     7:00p
SUPERCAL     <DIR>     5-06-86     7:21p
```

are separated by fences. As before, the output from DIR goes to FIND where the lines containing subdirectories are selected. The output from FIND goes to the SORT program where the lines are arranged in alphabetical order and displayed on the video screen. An example is shown in Figure 7.4.

SAVING TYPING WITH A BATCH FILE

You have seen that DOS programs have an extension of COM or EXE. But there is another type of program you can run. Files you create that contain regular keyboard commands are called *batch files* and have the extension BAT. Any command you can give to DOS from the keyboard can be placed into a batch file. When you give the primary name of the batch file, DOS executes the commands in that file as though you had typed the information from the keyboard.

A batch file can prepare your computer for your printer. For example, if you want to attach a serial printer that has a speed of 2400, you must give the commands

```
MODE  COM1:2400,N,8,1,P
MODE  LPT1:=COM1
```

Figure 7.4: *Sorted listing of subdirectories*

```
BASIC      <DIR>    4-30-86    8:03p
DOS        <DIR>    4-30-86    5:59p
EDIT       <DIR>    4-30-86    7:03p
FORTRAN    <DIR>    4-30-86    8:03p
INSTALL    <DIR>    4-30-86    8:56p
LETTERS    <DIR>    4-30-86    8:18p
PASCAL     <DIR>    4-30-86    9:04p
PROGRAMS   <DIR>    5-01-86    10:28a
REPORTS    <DIR>    5-05-86    8:44p
SIDEWAYS   <DIR>    5-06-86    6:45p
LOTUS      <DIR>    4-30-86    9:08p
SUPERCAL   <DIR>    5-06-86    7:21p
TK         <DIR>    4-30-86    8:53p
TOPVIEW    <DIR>    5-06-86    7:00p
```

each time you turn on or restart your computer. If you want to change to a parallel printer, you must give the command

    MODE LPT1:

You can place the first two commands into a file called SERIAL.BAT (or 2400.BAT) and put the third command into a file called PARALLEL.BAT. Then to change to the parallel printer, give the command

    PARALLEL

and you can change to the serial printer with the command

    SERIAL

A batch file can contain a replaceable parameter (sometimes called a *dummy parameter*). Then you can change the operation of a batch file by changing the parameter. We will consider dummy parameters in the next section.

USING A BATCH FILE TO LIST AND SORT

You can easily obtain a sorted list of your subdirectories by using a batch file. This will reduce the amount of typing that you have to do. Let's make such a batch file.

1. Go to your hard disk with the command

        C:

2. Make the root directory current with the command

        CD\

3. Create a batch file named FDIR.BAT (for find directory). You can use an editor such as EDLIN for this step. However, since this file has only one line, you can easily create it with the COPY command by typing

        COPY CON FDIR.BAT

Include spaces after COPY and CON but nowhere else. Press

Return. (You created the file SAMPLE.TXT in Chapter 3 with this technique.)

4. Type the line

    DIR *. ¦FIND "<DIR>" ¦SORT

    If you make a mistake, press the Backspace key. Be careful to include spaces after the commands DIR and FIND. Spaces may also be placed on either side of the fences, but they are not required. Then press Return.

5. Give the command

    ^Z

    and press Return. This terminates the COPY command and returns you to DOS.

6. Now, to obtain a sorted list of subdirectories, all you have to do is run the program by typing

    FDIR

7. To get a printed listing, turn on your printer and press ^P before giving the FDIR command. (You cannot use the > redirection symbol because there are three commands on one line.) Press ^P again after the listing is complete.

SEARCHING THROUGH ALL THE SUBDIRECTORIES

If after seeing the sorted list of subdirectories you still can't find where your program is located, you can try a different technique.

1. Go to the DOS subdirectory.

2. Then create the file named WHEREIS.BAT with the COPY command:

    COPY   CON   WHEREIS.BAT

3. Type the line

    CHKDSK /V ¦ FIND   "%1"

Place a space after FIND. The space after CHKDSK is optional since the slash also serves as a blank. Then press Return.

4. Close the file with the command

^Z

and press Return. This terminates the COPY command and returns you to DOS.

Your new file has one line but two commands. The first command runs the CHKDSK program with /V switch. The switch tells CHKDSK to list all files on the disk and include the subdirectory names. The output from CHKDSK usually appears on the video screen. However, in this example, the fence sends the output into the FIND program. The %1 symbol is a dummy parameter. DOS replaces it with the parameter you give to the batch-file command line. Let us see how it works.

Suppose, for example, you want to locate the file named REPORT.WK1. You can search for a part of the name, say REPORT. Give the DOS command

WHEREIS REPORT

The parameter, REPORT, must be given in uppercase. It replaces the %1 in the program, therefore, DOS converts your command to

CHKDSK /V ¦ FIND "REPORT"

Notice that the characters reported to FIND are enclosed with quotation marks. However, you did not place quotation marks around the file name on the command line. The batch file added them for you.

If files named REPORT.WK1 and REPORT.BAK are located in the subdirectory WORK, you will see the lines:

C:\WORK\REPORT.WK1
C:\WORK\REPORT.BAK

displayed on your video screen because these names contain the word REPORT. If there are other files with the letters REPORT, WHEREIS will find them too. For example, if a file named REPORT2.WK1 is located in subdirectory MONTHLY, you will also see the following line on your screen:

C:\MONTHLY\REPORT2.WK1

There is one potential problem with this program. You have seen that the letters on a command line can be given in either uppercase or lowercase. However, this is an exception. You must type the characters that you're searching for (REPORT in this example) in uppercase, or you will not find them. Of course, you can use only a part of the file name as a parameter.

FINDING A FILE FROM ITS CONTENTS

In the previous section you wrote a batch file that locates a file when you have forgotten the name of the subdirectory. In this section you will learn how to find the name of a file by its contents. This can be used when you forget the name of the file but not the name of the sub-directory. Alternatively, you may want to search a group of files for a particular word. For example, you might have a set of reports named REP-JAN, REP-FEB, and so on. (When you have a 30MB disk, it is easy to lose things.)

You cannot give the command

```
FIND "word" REP-*
```

because the FIND command does not accept wild cards for the file name. However, it is possible to write a batch file that does allow you to use wild cards for the file name.

1. Create a new disk file named LOCATE.BAT by giving the command

   ```
   COPY CON LOCATE.BAT
   ```

2. Type the line

   ```
   FOR %%X IN (%2) DO FIND %1 %%X
   ```

   putting a space after each word. Then press Return.

3. Give the command

   ```
   ^Z
   ```

   and press Return. This terminates the COPY command and returns you to DOS.

4. Give the command:

   ```
   WHEREIS SAMPLE.TXT
   ```

to find the directory that contains the file SAMPLE.TXT that you wrote in Chapter 4. Make that directory current.

5. Give the command

        LOCATE   "second"   SAMPLE.*

to search the files SAMPLE.TXT and SAMPLE.BAK for the word *second*. Of course, files named SAMPLE and SAM-PLE.PRN will also be searched if they are present. The word enclosed in quotation marks must agree exactly with the word you want to find. DOS replaces the second parameter, SAM-PLE.* with each file name that matches and then issues the command. The first time, the command might be

      FIND "second" SAMPLE.TXT

and the second time it might be

      FIND "second" SAMPLE.BAK

Each file name that matches the second parameter will be iden-tified on the screen such as

      – – – – – SAMPLE.TXT

and then each line of the file that contains the word *second* will be displayed on the screen. For example, you might see

      This is the second line.

The symbol %%X appears in two places of the batch file. DOS repeatedly replaces this symbol with each file name that matches the second parameter. The FIND command following DO is then repeatedly issued with each file name that matches.

HOW TO FREEZE THE SCREEN WITH THE MORE PROGRAM

You have seen that when information is rapidly scrolling on the video screen, it may disappear off the top before you have time to read it. The /P switch used with the DIR command, stops the scrolling each time the screen is filled. Then you can press any key to see the next screen. A similar feature is available for other programs through use of the MORE filter. Let's try out this program:

1. Give the command

    MORE <SAMPLE.TXT

    DOS displays the contents of the file named SAMPLE.TXT on the video screen. However, unlike the TYPE command, MORE stops the scrolling when the screen is filled. Press the space bar to see the next screen.

The MORE filter can also be fed from the output of another program by using a fence. For example, if you run CHKDSK with the /V switch, the output is longer than the screen. You can use MORE to stop the display when the screen is filled. Use the following command:

    CHKDSK /V ¦ MORE

When the /V parameter is given, CHKDSK displays the name of each file on the disk, including the DOS hidden files. However, the MORE program stops the display when the screen fills and gives the message

    – More –

Press any key to see the next screen.

HOW TO CHANGE THE DISK NAME
WITH THE LABEL PROGRAM

When you formatted a disk with the FORMAT program, you included the /V switch so you could assign a name or volume label to the disk. However, if you didn't include the /V switch when a disk was formatted, and you decide later that you need a volume name, or if you did assign one but you want to change it, you can assign a new one with the LABEL program.

To change the name of the disk in drive B, give the command

    LABEL B:

and you will be asked to type the new label. As with the FORMAT program, you can use up to 11 characters, including blanks, underlines, and minus signs. Then press the Return key. For example, the name

    DOS 3-1

is acceptable. The new name will show when you give the DIR command.

HOW TO CHANGE THE DRIVE LETTER

You have seen that drives A and B are floppy disks and drive C is a hard disk or RAM disk. However, it is possible to change the drive designation. Let's see why you would want to do that.

Some programs will only run on a particular drive, say A, and expect to find their data on another drive, say B. However, if you have a hard disk or RAM disk that is drive C, it would be more convenient to run the program from drive C. You can temporarily define this drive to be A and B also. Then the program can run entirely on drive C.

1. If you have a C drive, go there with the command

    C:

2. Give the command

    ASSIGN A = C

   to temporarily define drive A as drive C. (Drive C continues to also be drive C at the same time. That is, the ASSIGN command does not change the second drive in the command, only the first.)

3. Give the command

    DIR A:

   and notice that drive A does not start up but instead you get a listing of the files on your hard disk.

4. Give the command

    DIR C:

   and see that the result is the same as the previous command.

5. Type the command

    ASSIGN

with no parameters, to return drive A to its original definition.

You cannot define both drive A and drive B with two commands such as

    ASSIGN A = C

and

    ASSIGN B = C

because each ASSIGN command cancels the previous one. Thus after these two commands have been given, drive C responds to requests for both drive B and drive C. However, drive A is normal. If you want to change two drives at once, both must be included in the same command. Thus the command

    ASSIGN A = C;B = C

makes drive C respond to requests for all three drives: A, B, and C. This command must have exactly one space; it is placed between ASSIGN and A.

SUMMARY

In this chapter you have explored the DOS external programs ATTRIB, COMP, FIND, MORE, LABEL, and ASSIGN. ATTRIB can guard against accidental file erasure; COMP compares two files to see if they are the same; FIND locates words; MORE freezes the screen when it becomes full; and LABEL changes the name assigned to a disk. You wrote two short batch programs that can list the subdirectories in alphabetical order and another to find a disk file that contains a particular word. ASSIGN allows you to run floppy disk programs on drive C.

8 Copying Files

COPY is a built-in DOS command that can be used for copying files and transferring information to and from peripherals. We previously used COPY to copy files from one disk to another. We also used COPY to create a disk file from information you typed at the keyboard and to send a disk file to the printer. Because COPY is such an important utility program, this entire chapter is devoted to it.

COPY is primarily a file transfer program. As its name suggests, it is used to transfer information from one device, such as a disk, to another, such as another disk or peripheral. COPY can:

- Copy a single file from one disk to another
- Copy a group of files from one disk to another
- Copy all files from one disk to another
- Copy a file and change its name
- Join several files into a single file
- Create a new file from the keyboard
- Send a file to the printer

Although you may think you need only a few of COPY's capabilities, it is important to know what features are available. Therefore, you should read through this chapter completely, and then go back and study in detail the sections of specific interest to you.

HOW TO TURN ON VERIFICATION

You learned earlier that when DOS copies a file, it does not check to see that the new file has been correctly made unless you have turned on the verification feature. Therefore, you should give the command

    VERIFY ON

each time you turn on or reset the computer. It is possible to give this command from the keyboard. However, it is easier to place this command into your AUTOEXEC.BAT file, which is automatically read by DOS whenever the computer is turned on.

HOW TO COPY A FILE

The most important feature of COPY is the duplication of a file from one disk to another. As you have learned, COPY can duplicate a single file or a group of files with one command.

COPYING ONE FILE

The COPY command can duplicate a file and make a new one with a different name on the same disk or the same name on a different disk. Suppose, for example, that you want to write a letter or report that is similar to one you wrote previously. You can save some typing by making a copy of the original and then making changes on the copy. The copy must have a different file name (if you want to keep the original, too). Suppose the original file is named SAMPLE.TXT and the new file is to be named SIMPLE.TAX.

1. Make your system disk current.

2. Give the command:

    COPY SAMPLE.TXT SIMPLE.TAX

Because COPY is a built-in command, you do not have to look for it on one of your disks. This command contains two parameters—the first is the name of the original file and the second is the name of the new file.

As you have seen, parameters must be separated from the command and from each other by at least one space.

In this example both the original file and the new file are on the same disk—the current disk. When a file name refers to the current drive, you may omit the drive name in the COPY command. There is no harm in including the drive name when you refer to the default drive, but it is not necessary. On the other hand, the drive name must be included when the file is not on the default drive. Consider, for example, the command

COPY A:SAMPLE.TXT B:SIMPLE.TAX

It copies the file SAMPLE.TXT from drive A to drive B. Because both drives are specified, it does not matter what the current drive is.

The two previous examples do two things at once—copy a file and change its name. If you want the new file to have the same name as the original file, you can simplify the command by omitting the second name. However, you must give the drive name for the new file. For example, the command:

COPY A:SAMPLE.TXT B:

copies the file SAMPLE.TXT from drive A to drive B. It does the same thing as the command   .

COPY A:SAMPLE.TXT B:SAMPLE.TXT

but it is shorter.

If the original file is on the default drive, you can omit the drive name from the first parameter:

COPY SAMPLE.TXT B:

Finally, if the original file is not on the current drive and you want to create the new file on the current drive, you can omit the second parameter. For example, the command

COPY A:SAMPLE.TXT

copies a file from drive A to the current drive. This is the most useful form for copying a file because only one parameter is required. (The second parameter is implied.)

There cannot be two files with the same name on the same disk. Therefore if drive A is current and you give the command

    COPY A:SAMPLE.TXT

COPY does not carry out the command. Instead, it gives the following error message:

    File cannot be copied onto itself

COPYING SEVERAL FILES AT ONCE

In the previous section, the COPY command only copied one file at a time because you gave DOS specific file names. However, it is frequently convenient to copy several files at once.

Remember in Chapter 3, you copied all the files on disk A over to disk B with the command

    COPY A:*.* B:

When a parameter to the COPY command contains the wild-card symbols ? or *, all files that match the specification will be copied. The question mark matches any one character, including a blank, in the given position. The asterisk tells COPY to interpret the remainder of the field (either the primary name or the extension) as though it were filled with question marks.

When there is a wild-card character in the first parameter to COPY, the second parameter should either be a drive name or it should be omitted to indicate the current drive. For example, the command

    COPY A:MEMO?.*

copies all files matching the wild-card file name from drive A to the current drive. File names that match this parameter contain the four letters MEMO and no more than one additional character in the primary name. For example, the file names MEMO.TXT, MEMO.BAK, MEMO2.TXT, and MEMO match the wild-card name MEMO?.*.

When a parameter contains wild cards, the name of each file that matches the parameter is displayed on the video screen as it is copied. If no file matches the parameter, you will see the following message:

    0 file(s) copied

You will need four files to practice with; create them now with COPY. Since you are going to use only the file names, not the contents of these files, it does not matter what they contain. Therefore, you can simply duplicate the file named SAMPLE.TXT that you made in Chapters 3 and 4.

1. Go to your disk that has the file SAMPLE.TXT.

2. Give the following commands:

   ```
   COPY  SAMPLE.TXT  SALES1.WK1
   COPY  SAMPLE.TXT  SALES2.WK1
   COPY  SAMPLE.TXT  SALES3.WK1
   COPY  SAMPLE.TXT  SALES44.WK1
   ```

   Remember, you can use F3 and Backspace to reduce the amount of typing. That is, after completing the first line, press F3 to repeat it. Then press the Backspace key five times. Change the 1 to 2 and then press the F3 key again. For the last file, press Ins to insert the second 4.

3. After you have created these four files, check the directory with the command:

   ```
   DIR SALES*.WK1
   ```

   You should now see a listing of the four new files like the one shown in Figure 8.1. The number of bytes should be the same since they are copies of SAMPLE.TXT.

4. Make your hard disk the current drive. If you do not have a hard disk, put a formatted disk in drive B and make it current.

5. Give the command

   ```
   COPY A:SALES?.WK1
   ```

   Notice that there is only one parameter to COPY and that parameter does not refer to the current drive. This command copies three of the four new files. The video screen will look like Figure 8.2. DOS only copies three of the four files because the fourth file, SALES44.WK1, does not match the wild-card name SALES?.WK1.

Figure 8.1: *Directory listing of four new files*

```
Volume in drive A is DOS 3-2
Directory of  A:\

SALES1   WK1     256   9-01-86    9:20p
SALES2   WK1     256   9-01-86    9:20p
SALES3   WK1     256   9-01-86    9:20p
SALES44  WK1     256   9-01-86    9:20p
        4 File(s)    32922 bytes free
```

Figure 8.2: *Copying files with a wild card*

```
C:SALES1.WK1
C:SALES2.WK1
C:SALES3.WK1
        3 File(s) copied
```

The other wild-card symbol, the asterisk, matches any combination of characters in the remainder of its field, regardless of the length. Internally, DOS expands the * symbol to a string of question marks. For example, you can transfer all four of the previous files with the command

```
COPY  A:SALES*.WK1
```

As another example, assume drive A contains the files:

```
SALES1.WK1
SALES2.WK1
LETTER.TXT
MEMO.PRN
SALES1.BAK
```

The ambiguous name *.WK1 matches the files:

```
SALES1.WK1
SALES2.WK1
```

and the name SALES1.* matches the files:

```
SALES1.WK1
SALES1.BAK
```

As you already know, the expression *.* matches all the files in the directory.

COPYING FILES WITH A HARD DISK

Because a hard disk is so large, it should be organized into subdirectories chosen by subject. To copy a file from a floppy disk in drive A to the hard disk follow these steps:

1. Go to the hard disk with

```
C:
```

2. Go to the desired subdirectory. For example, the command

```
CD\DOS
```

changes to the subdirectory named DOS.

3. Give the command

COPY A:SAMPLE.TXT

to copy a file from drive A onto the current directory of drive C.

To copy the other way, from the hard disk to a floppy:

1. Go to the hard disk.

2. Change the current subdirectory to the one containing the file you want to copy.

3. Put the floppy disk into drive A and make it the current drive with the command

A:

4. Give the command

COPY C:SAMPLE.TXT

Notice that this form of the COPY command is similar to the previous one. Only the drive name is different. Thus, the current subdirectory on a hard disk is referenced as drive C.

If you want to copy a file from one subdirectory to another on the hard disk, make the destination directory current. Then COPY only needs one parameter. For example, let's copy SAMPLE.TXT from subdirectory DOS to the root directory:

1. Go to the hard disk with the command

C:

2. Make the root directory current with the command

CD\

3. Now type

COPY   \DOS\SAMPLE.TXT

Notice that this command has the same format as the others in this chapter. You make the destination directory current. Then you only have to give one parameter to the COPY command. Of course, you can copy a group of files from one subdirectory to another. For example, the command

```
COPY \DOS\SALES*.WK1
```

copies all the files that match the wild-card symbol from subdirectory DOS to the current directory.

In the three previous examples you copied files into the current subdirectory from another subdirectory. Only one parameter is needed with this method. Of course, you can copy in the other direction: from the current directory to another subdirectory. Then you must give two parameters. However, you must be very careful not to lose files or create files where you do not expect them to be. Let us see how.

The command

```
COPY *.WK1 \EDIT\*.*
```

copies all files that have the extension WK1 from the current directory to the subdirectory named EDIT. You can shorten this command to

```
COPY *.WK1 \EDIT
```

However, you should avoid this shortened form because the second parameter, \EDIT, can have two meanings. If the subdirectory named EDIT exists, then this command will do the same thing as the previous one. However, if the subdirectory EDIT does not exist (or you misspelled the name) the COPY command will combine all files that match the wild-card name into one file and name that file EDIT in the root directory. If there was originally a file by that name, it would be deleted. Furthermore, if you now give the command

```
DEL *.WK1
```

because you think you have another copy in subdirectory EDIT, you will lose everything.

A similar problem can occur with single file names. For example, the command

```
COPY SALES1.WK1 \EDIT
```

can also have two meanings. If there is a subdirectory named EDIT, and it is not the current directory, this command will do what you want. It will make a copy of SALES1.WK1 in subdirectory EDIT. However, if a subdirectory named EDIT does not already exist, this command will create a *file* named EDIT on the current disk. It will be a copy of the file named SALES1.WK1.

HOW TO CONCATENATE FILES

Sometimes you need to combine two or more files into a new file. This process is called *concatenation.* When you are concatenating files, you have to take into account that there are two different types of disk files: text and non-text.

TEXT AND NON-TEXT FILES

Text files are written by you and can be documents such as letters, reports, and computer programs. They can be created with a text editor such as EDLIN. Text files are made up of letters; digits; special symbols such as $,%,&, and *; and certain control characters such as Return, the tab key, and the Backspace character. (They are all ASCII characters and are identified in Appendix C.) DOS puts the ^ Z symbol at the end of every text file to mark the end of the text; therefore, no text may extend beyond a ^ Z and ^ Z cannot be used as a valid character within a text file.

Non-text, or binary files, such as those with COM or EXE extensions, are different from text files in that they can contain every possible combination of characters, including the ^ Z character. As a result, ^ Z cannot mark the end of a non-text file. (The file length is specified in the directory.) The COPY command copies every file as though it were a non-text file and the presence or lack of a ^ Z has no effect. However, when concatenating files, COPY assumes it is working with text files and stops when it finds a ^ Z. Therefore, the concatenation of text files must be handled a little differently from the concatenation of non-text files.

CONCATENATING TEXT FILES

The plus symbol (+) is placed between file names you want to concatenate. That is why you cannot use this symbol in a file name. The following is an example of a concatenation command:

COPY SALES1.WK1 + SALES2.WK1 SALESALL

This command creates the file SALESALL by combining the two files
SALES1.WK1 and SALES2.WK1. The first parameter is

SALES1.WK1 + SALES2.WK1

It contains two file names connected with a plus symbol. Blanks may be
placed on either side of the plus symbol for legibility. In this example,
the two original files and the new file are on the default drive, therefore
no drive names need to be included in the command. After concatenation, the two original files still exist unchanged. You must be sure that
there is room on the disk for the new file as well as the original files.

    After concatenation, the new file contains the text of the first file
up to but not including its ^Z character, followed by the text of the second file. Thus, the information in the new file appears in the exact order
of the file names in the first parameter.

    You can concatenate more than two files by including additional
file names, each separated from the next by a plus symbol. For
example, the following command joins three text files:

COPY SALES1.WK1 + SALES2.WK1 + SALES3.WK1 SALESALL

Again, all files in this example are on the default drive.

    You can concatenate files from different disks by including drive
names with the file names. For example, the command

COPY A:PART1.TXT + B:PART2.TXT + B:PART3.TXT BIG.TXT

combines one file from drive A and two files from drive B into a new file
on the current drive.

    Sometimes it is necessary to append one or two files to the end of
another file. That is, you want the combined file to take the name of one
of the original files. Since two files cannot have the same name, the original file must be erased. For example, the command

COPY FIRST + SECOND + THIRD FIRST

combines the files FIRST, SECOND, and THIRD into a temporary file. If
the concatenation is successful, the original file named FIRST is

deleted, and the concatenated version is given the original name FIRST. The files SECOND and THIRD continue to exist after the concatenation. Furthermore, the second parameter can be omitted, because it is the same as the first file name of the first parameter.

INSERTING CHARACTERS DURING CONCATENATION

It is possible to insert characters from the keyboard during a concatenation step. Then you can add a message marking the boundary of each part of your new combined file. For example, suppose you give the command

```
COPY  SALES1 + CON + SALES2 + CON + SALES3  NEW
```

This command directs COPY to create the file NEW, beginning with the existing file SALES1. CON is a reference to your keyboard. Therefore, the CON parameter tells COPY to read any characters you type from the keyboard, and place them in the new file. Of course, you can make corrections with the backspace key while you are entering text. You signal the end of the keyboard entry by typing ^Z and pressing Return. COPY then copies SALES2, the next parameter, to the new file. The second CON tells COPY to read characters from the keyboard until you type another ^Z and Return. Finally, COPY copies SALES3 to the new file.

COPY displays the name of each file as it is added to the new file. When you see the word CON on the screen, it is your turn to type. The characters you enter from the keyboard are displayed on the video screen as you type them. When you type ^Z and Return, the next file name appears.

ADDING TEXT TO AN EXISTING FILE WITH COPY

You have learned how to create a disk file from information typed at the keyboard and how to combine information from an existing file and from the keyboard. With these techniques you can easily add information to the end of an existing disk file. For example, suppose that you want to add a line of text to the end of your AUTOEXEC.BAT file. Give the command

```
COPY  AUTOEXEC.BAT + CON
```

The COPY command will prepare a new file that is a duplicate of the original. The name

AUTOEXEC.BAT

appears as this file is copied to the new version. You see

CON

when it is your turn to type. When you type ⌃ Z and press the Return key, the text you typed will be appended to the end of the new file that will become AUTOEXEC.BAT. Notice that in this example, the new file has the same name as the original. This is acceptable when CON is the final name in the list to be concatenated.

If you want to add information to the beginning of the file rather than the end, give the command

COPY CON + AUTOEXEC.BAT AUTOEXEC.NEW

reversing the two parts of the first parameter and adding a different second parameter. (Do not use the same file name for both parts when CON is placed first or you will lose your file.)

CONCATENATING FILES WITH WILD CARDS

You can concatenate files with wild cards. For example, the command

COPY S∗.WK1 BIG

creates a file named BIG that contains all files that match the wild-card parameter S∗.WK1. However, this is not a very useful command, because DOS will combine the files in whatever order it finds them in the directory. If you want them in a particular order you must list each one explicitly in the first parameter. However, this command does let you print a group of files with a single command. For example, the command:

COPY F∗.∗ PRN

will print all files whose names begin with F.

CONCATENATING NON-TEXT FILES

When COPY encounters a ^Z character during a concatenation step, it assumes that it has found the end of the file. However, as you have seen, ^Z does not mark the end of a non-text file.

The way to solve this concatenation problem is to add the /B (for binary) switch after names of non-text files. If you want to concatenate both non-text files with text files, you can place the /A (for ASCII) switch after the names of text files. For example, look at the command:

    COPY FIRST.COM/B + SECOND.ASC/A COMBIN.BOT/B

This command combines the non-text file named FIRST.COM with the text file named SECOND.ASC to create the non-text file named COMBIN.BOT.

You must not give the /B parameter when concatenating text files or they will be incorrectly joined. On the other hand, it is not necessary to use the /A parameter for concatenating text files and you do not need to use either switch when simply copying single files.

HOW TO TRANSFER A DISK FILE TO A PERIPHERAL DEVICE

The COPY command provides general-purpose transfer capabilities that allow a file to be copied not only from disk to disk, but also between various devices such as the keyboard, video screen, printer, and phone modem. Let us consider this mode of transfer.

CREATING A FILE WITH COPY

In previous chapters you created disk files from information you typed from the keyboard. In Chapter 2, you did this with the command

    COPY CON SAMPLE.TXT

(If you did not create this file in Chapter 3, please refer to that chapter and do so now. You will work with this file in the following section.)

The first parameter of this command, CON, refers not to a disk file but to the keyboard. (CON is a reserved word and you cannot use it for a file name.) The second parameter, SAMPLE.TXT, is the name of the new disk file.

When you give this command, COPY reads each character typed at the keyboard and enters it into the disk file named SAMPLE.TXT. Press ^Z and Return to complete the operation. This COPY command is useful for creating short files.

PRINTING A FILE WITH COPY

You have seen that there are several possible ways to obtain a printed listing of a text file. The simplest method, which was discussed in Chapters 2 and 3, is to engage the printer with ^P and then give the TYPE command. Another way is to use COPY. The command

    COPY SAMPLE.TXT PRN

sends the disk file SAMPLE.TXT to the printer.

Of course, all the regular COPY features apply when you use COPY to print a file. Several files can be concatenated and printed with a single command. For example, the command

    COPY SALES1 + SALES2 + SALES3 PRN

prints the three files SALES1, SALES2, and SALES3. If you do not have a printer, you can try out this command by substituting the video screen. Give the command

    COPY SALES1 + SALES2 + SALES3 CON

and the three files will appear on the video screen.

HOW TO COPY READ-ONLY FILES

You learned in Chapter 7 that you can mark a file as read-only by using the program ATTRIB. Then the file cannot be deleted with the DEL command. If you copy a write-protected file to another disk, the new copy will be identical to the original except for one thing: the copy will not be write-protected and can be deleted with the DEL command. If you want to protect the copy, you must change its status with the ATTRIB program.

On the other hand, if you try to copy a file to a disk that already has a write-protected file with the same name, the copy will not be performed. As an example, suppose you write-protect the file named

SALES1.WK1 that is on the current drive. Then if you try to copy another version from drive A with the command

    COPY   A:SALES1.WK1

COPY will not perform the transfer because it would have to erase the original version and that version has the read-only attribute set. Instead, COPY responds with this cryptic error message:

    File creation error
    0 file(s) copied

If the existing file named SALES1.WK1 did not have the read-only attribute set, COPY would have automatically deleted the original version and replaced it with the copy.

HOW TO CHANGE THE FILE CREATION DATE

As you have seen, the current date and time are recorded in the directory when a file is first created. However, when you later copy a file, the original creation date and time are repeated in the new copy.

If you want the time and date in your file to reflect the time of the copy, it is possible to change it with the COPY command by playing a trick. (You can temporarily change the system clock to any convenient value before you do this trick. Then you can change it back afterward.) You can change the creation date and time to the current value for a file on the current drive with a command you used earlier:

    COPY   MYFILE +,,

This command tells COPY to concatenate the file MYFILE with nothing and call the result MYFILE. Since a file made by concatenation is new, COPY gives it a new date and time. This technique works satisfactorily for text files. However, there is a potential problem for non-text files.

As you saw previously, you must use the /B switch when concatenating non-text files. Therefore, to change the creation date and time for a binary file, use the command:

    COPY   MYFILE.COM/B +,,

SUMMARY

COPY is a powerful general-purpose file-transfer program. Though it is most often used for simple disk-to-disk transfers, it can do much more. In this chapter you learned how to transfer files between devices and disks, transfer several files at once, join several files into a new file, and change the creation date and time.

9 Resident Utility Programs

In the previous chapters you studied the details of DOS commands and programs and you learned how to configure your computer so it will do things your way. However, we have confined the discussion to DOS system programs, programs that make your computer operate. In this chapter you will look at resident utility programs that can make your computer easier to use. In particular, we will consider SideKick, a program you can purchase. Once installed, a resident program continues to work while you run other programs. Let us see how this type of program integrates with DOS.

You run an ordinary computer program by typing its name and pressing the Return key. Then DOS copies the program into memory and starts it up. When the program is finished, DOS recovers the memory space used by the program so it can be assigned to the next program. However, resident utility programs are a little different. You run them in the usual way, by typing their name. However, when the program returns control to DOS, it does not release its memory. Rather, it stays in memory and continues to operate in *background* mode. Therefore, this type of program is known as a *memory-resident program*. A memory-resident program reduces the memory space available to other programs but in return, it remains active, working all the time. The RAM disk program, VDISK, is a memory-resident program that creates an electronic disk that you can use at any time, and the print buffer program, SUPERSPL, allows you to continue with other tasks while the printer is working. We will now consider another memory-resident program, SideKick.

HOW TO ADD POWER
TO YOUR COMPUTER WITH SIDEKICK

The popular memory-resident program, SideKick, allows you to work with a calendar, calculator, ASCII table, and notepad while you are running another program. The main program is named SK.COM and the help file is called SK.HLP. Your SideKick program may also include files named README.COM and READ-ME.SK that contain information not found in the users' manual. The complete SideKick program will reduce your usable memory size about 64K bytes. If you cannot spare that much memory, you can load one of the smaller versions that do not have all the features.

One version, SKN, omits the calendar and saves you about 5K bytes. Another version, SKC, omits the notepad, saving you about 12K bytes. Finally there is SKM, which omits the notepad, calculator, and dialer to save you 22K bytes.

If you have a hard disk, you can transfer the SideKick files to a separate subdirectory as follows:

1. Go to the root directory of your hard disk with the commands

    ```
    C:
    CD\
    ```

2. Create a subdirectory called SK with the command

    ```
    MD  SK
    ```

3. Go there with the command

    ```
    CD  SK
    ```

4. Put the original SideKick disk in drive A and copy the SideKick files to the hard disk with the commands

    ```
    COPY  A:SK.*
    COPY  A:SKINST.*
    ```

5. Go to the subdirectory that contains your DOS programs:

    ```
    CD\DOS
    ```

6. Create a batch file named SK.BAT. (Be sure that SideKick is not in this directory.) You can use COPY by giving the command

   ```
   COPY  CON  SK.BAT
   ```

   or your can use an editor such as EDLIN. Give the command

   ```
   EDLIN  SK.BAT
   ```

7. Add the five lines:

   ```
   C:
   CD\SK
   SK
   CLS
   CD\
   ```

   The first line makes the hard disk current, the second line changes to the SK subdirectory, the third line loads SideKick, the fourth line clears the screen, and the last line makes the root directory of the hard disk current. This unusual technique is necessary because SideKick must be loaded from the current directory. But you do not normally want the SideKick subdirectory to be current. With this batch file in your program subdirectory, you can run SideKick from any disk or directory. If you find that you always want to use SideKick, place the SK command last in your AUTOEXEC.BAT file.

8. If you have a floppy-disk system, you can make a backup copy of SideKick and then give the SK command while the backup copy is the current disk.

9. If you have set up a RAM disk with your floppy-disk system, put the SideKick disk in drive B. Then copy SK.COM and SK.HLP to your system disk in A with the command

   ```
   COPY  B:SK.*
   ```

   And put the following lines in your AUTOEXEC.BAT file:

   ```
   COPY  SK.HLP  C:>NUL
   C:
   A:SK
   A:
   ```

That way the help file can be quickly read when needed.

INSTALLING SIDEKICK

When you install SideKick, you can change it so it performs better on your system by adjusting the screen flicker and color mode. If you have a non-IBM video adapter, perform this test to see if you need to adjust SideKick: At the DOS command, hold the Return key down until the DOS prompts scroll off the top of the screen. See if the video screen flickers. The default of the SideKick installation program is set to compensate for the flicker that occurs with an IBM system. If your screen flickers, then you can use SideKick without change. However, if your screen does not flicker, you should run the installation program and change the default to get maximum performance out of SideKick.

You learned previously that several different types of screens can be used with your computer. If you have a black-and-white graphics screen, you should run the installation program to turn off the color mode. If you do not turn off the color mode, the screen will be impossible to read.

You can change either feature or both of them with the installation program. To run this program follow the steps below.

1. Go to the SideKick subdirectory with the command

   CD\SK

2. Run the installation program with the command

   SKINST

   You are given the choice of seven features to install (Figure 9.1).

3. Press S to select the screen type. You are given a choice of the default display or three other types of displays (Figure 9.2).

4. Type 3 to select black-and-white graphics display and then Return if you have that type of screen. Otherwise, just press Return for no change.

5. The next question asks if your screen blinks when it scrolls. Press N if it does not or Y if it does. Then press Return.

Figure 9.1: *SideKick installation menu*

```
                Installation program for SideKick 1.50

            Choose installation item from the following:

    Screen type | notepad Commands | Notepad size | right Margin

    Dialer      | cOlors           | Activate commands


            Enter S, C, N, M, D, O, A or Q to quit:
```

Figure 9.2: *Screen menu for SideKick installation*

```
Choose one of the following displays:

   0)  Default display mode
   1)  Monochrome display    (includes Hercules card)
   2)  Color display 80x25
   3)  B/W   display 80x25  (one-color monitor connected to color graphics card)

Which display? (0-3 or ◄┘ for no change): 0

Does your screen blink when the text scrolls? (Y/N, ◄┘ for no change): N


Do you want to use Sidekick on top of graphics (Y/N, ◄┘ for no change): N
```

6. The third question asks if you want to use SideKick on top of graphics. If you only use text on your screen, just press Return.

7. You are now returned to the original menu. Press Q to quit and return to DOS.

You will not need the installation programs again unless you want to change the features. Therefore, they do not need to be on your hard disk or your system disk.

Resident programs monitor some of DOS's operations. If you have more than one resident program, there may be an interference if two are monitoring the same operation. The SideKick instruction manual tells you to load SideKick last to avoid a conflict. Therefore, run the RAM-disk program, the printer-buffer program, and any other resident programs first. Then run SideKick. Since the VDISK program must be run from the CONFIG.SYS file and the other resident programs can be run from the AUTOEXEC.BAT file, place the SK command at the end of the AUTOEXEC.BAT file.

Because SideKick is a memory-resident program, it quickly returns control to DOS after it is started up. However, from now on it will be working, monitoring the keyboard, and waiting for your commands. You can activate SideKick either at the DOS prompt or while any program that you may be running is waiting for keyboard input. For example, you can activate SideKick while you are creating a file with EDLIN.

SideKick is activated by pressing the Ctrl and Alt keys (^ Alt) simultaneously. This is called the *hot key*. You have seen that both the Ctrl and the Alt keys alter the meaning of other keys. Therefore, you normally would never press them at the same time. That is why these two keys were selected for SideKick. Let's try SideKick.

1. Give the command

   SK

2. Press the Ctrl and Alt keys simultaneously. A menu listing the features of SideKick appears (pops up) in the middle of the video screen (see Figure 9.3). Information that appears on your screen in this way is called a *window*. Any text that was on your screen is now covered by the window. However, it is not lost.

3. Press the Esc key and the SideKick menu disappears and the original information reappears. You can alternately press ^ Alt to pop-up the SideKick menu and Esc to remove it.

4. When the menu is present, press the ScrollLock key, then press the right-arrow key to move the SideKick window to the right. You can move the menu anywhere on the screen with the four cursor keys.

5. Press ScrollLock again to fix the window position. If you remove the window and then pop it up again, the window will return to wherever it was before you removed it.

You can see from the menu that there are seven features you can select. However, you are not limited to only one feature at a time. You can have several SideKick features present on the screen at once. You can select SideKick features in one of four ways: by pressing the indicated function key (F1–F7), selecting the mnemonic letter key that is highlighted, holding the Alt key and pressing the mnemonic letter key, or moving the cursor to the desired option and pressing Return.

If you want to install another resident program after SideKick has been run, you must remove SideKick first. To remove SideKick:

1. Activate SideKick with ^ Alt.

2. Press Ctrl-Home.

3. Press Ctrl-End.

Figure 9.3: *The SideKick main menu*

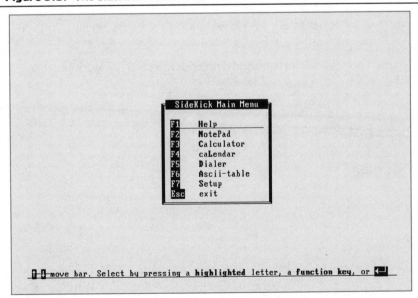

USING THE NOTEPAD

One of the choices in the SideKick main menu is a powerful text editor called the notepad. You can use it to create and alter short disk files such as your CONFIG.SYS and AUTOEXEC.BAT files. The benefit of the notepad is that while you are working in another program, or just giving commands to DOS, you can take notes or capture information on the screen.

The notepad commands are nearly identical to those of WordStar, although you can change them to something else if you want. Let's create a short text file:

1. Activate SideKick with ^ Alt.

2. Press N to display the notepad. The default file name C:\SK\NOTES is shown at the top of the window if the SK subdirectory is current. Otherwise, the current directory name will be given.

3. Press the F3 key to select a new file name. (The bottom line identifies the F3 key with the words *new file* when the notepad is active.)

4. Type the name

   SAMPLE2.TXT

   It is not necessary to delete the original name because it disappears when you begin typing.

5. Type ^ QT. The time and date appear in the notepad like this:

   20:42:13 10/8/1986

   Press Return to start the next line.

6. Type the following two lines:

   This is the second line of my Sidekick file.
   This is the third line of my Sidekick file.

Moving Around Your File

So far, the SideKick notepad looks a little like EDLIN without the line numbers. But the notepad is a full-screen editor, like WordStar. This means that you can easily move around on the screen if you want to make changes. Follow the steps below to learn how to move around the notepad.

1. Press F1 and you will see a help window that identifies some of the notepad commands like the one shown in Figure 9.4.

2. Press the down-arrow to see the next help window. (The commands shown in the help windows are also given inside the back cover of the SideKick manual.)

3. Press Esc to exit from the help window.

4. Move the cursor to the second line of your file by pressing the up-arrow key twice.

5. Press the Home key if the cursor is not at the beginning of the line.

6. Press the right-arrow key. The cursor now moves right one character at a time.

7. Hold the Ctrl key and press the right-arrow again. Now the cursor jumps right one word at a time rather than one character at a time.

8. Hold the Ctrl key and press the left-arrow. The cursor jumps left one word at a time.

9. Press the End key to move the cursor to the end of the line.

Before going any farther, you should learn how to stop the notepad if it is doing the wrong thing. The notepad panic button is ^U; it is like the ^Break command of EDLIN. When you give this command, the notepad stops what it is doing and returns control to you.

Expanding Your File

To enlarge the notepad file, follow these steps:

1. Use the up or down arrow to place the cursor on the second line.

2. Press the Home key to put the cursor at the beginning of the line.

3. Press ^KB to mark the beginning of a block of text. (The second character of a two-letter command like this one can be given in any of three ways—lowercase, uppercase, or with the Ctrl key pressed.)

4. Move beyond the last line of text by pressing

   ^PgDn

   The cursor should be at the beginning of the line after your last
   line. If instead the cursor is on the last line of text, press End and
   then Return.

5. Press ^KK. The two lines change to show that you have marked
   a block of text. You can do several things with a marked block.
   You can move it, delete it, write it as a separate disk file, trans-
   port it into another program, print it, sort the lines, or duplicate
   it. For now we're going to copy it.

6. Give the command ^KC to copy the first two lines.

7. Type ^KC again and there will be six lines.

8. Press ^KH and the two marked lines return to normal (H is the
   mnemonic for hide).

Using the Find and Replace Feature

1. Type ^PgUp to move the cursor to the beginning of the file.

Figure 9.4: *Help window for SideKick notepad*

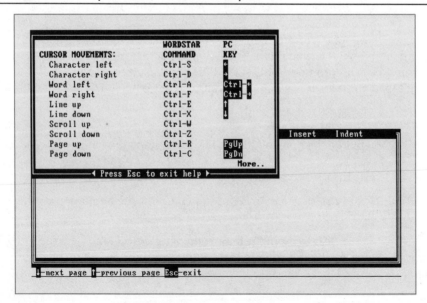

2. Let's change the fourth line from

    This is the second line of my Sidekick file.

to

    This is the fourth line of my Sidekick file.

Start by giving the command

    ^QA

This replacement command is like the R command of EDLIN.

3. The word

    Find:

appears at the top left corner of the notepad window. Type the word

    second

When you press Return, the words

    Replace with:

appear. Type the word

    fourth

and press Return.

4. Just press the Return key again in response to the next question:

    Options

The cursor moves to the first occurrence of the word *second.* SideKick then asks if you want to replace this word.

5. Type N for no because this is only the second line.

6. Press ^L to repeat the search. Now the cursor stops at the word *second* located on the fourth line.

7. You are again asked if you want to make a replacement. Press Y this time and the word will be changed.

If you want to search for a word, but not replace it, give the command ^QF (for find) rather than ^QA.

Inserting and Deleting Text

You have written text directly into the notepad and you have changed one word to another. However, it is also possible to write new text directly over the original text. This is a powerful feature of full screen editors. Let's try this out:

1. Move the cursor to the beginning of the file by typing ^PgUp.

2. Press the down-arrow key to move the cursor to the beginning of the second line. Notice the information at the top of the notepad window. The file name is shown on the left side. Then the line number (2) and column number (1) are given near the center. The word *Insert* should appear next. If the word *Overwrite* appears instead, press the Ins key.

3. Type the following:

   Something new is added

   Notice that the original text moves over as you type the new characters. The characters you type are inserted into the original text because SideKick is in insert mode.

4. Press the Ins key and watch the word *Insert* change to *Overwrite* on the top of the window. This shows that the notepad is now in overwrite mode.

5. Continue on the second line typing the words

   to my file

   Now, the characters you type are written over the original text, thereby erasing it.

There are many different ways to delete parts of your text. Let's try out a few:

1. Leaving your cursor where it was in the last step, type ^QY. The remaining text on the line is now deleted.

2. Press the Home key to move to the left side.

3. Press the down-arrow to move down one line.

4. Press ^T to delete the word the cursor is on.

5. Move over to the letter *r* in the word *third* and press the Del key. The character at the cursor position is deleted.

6. Press Backspace and the character to the left of the cursor is deleted.

7. Give the command

   ^Y

   to delete the entire line. The remaining lines move up.

8. Move to the center of the line by pressing ^right-arrow several times. Type ^N to split the current line in two at the cursor position.

9. Type ^T and the split line returns to its original form.

Using the Block Commands

You enlarged this notepad file with the block-copy command. Now let us consider the other SideKick block commands.

1. Go to the beginning of the file with

   ^PgUp

2. Give the beginning block command:

   ^KB

3. Move down one line with the down-arrow and give the end block command:

   ^KK

   The first line will be highlighted, showing that it is marked as a block.

4. To unmark the block, press ^KH. For now you want it marked so press ^KH again.

5. Give the command

   ^ KY

   to delete the marked block. This is a safer way to delete several lines of a file than using ^ Y. (If you accidently delete lines of your file by either method, you cannot get them back.)

Sorting Lines in Your File

SideKick can sort lines in alphabetical or numeric order. Let us see how.

1. Go to the end of the file with the command

   ^ PgDn

2. Check that Insert mode is current, not Overwrite. Press the Ins key if Overwrite is current.

3. Mark the beginning of the block with ^ KB.

4. Press Return.

5. Type the following six numbers:

   ```
   13
   26
   65
   11
   53
   27
   ```

   (Press Return after each line.)

6. Mark the block end with ^ KK. The appearance of the block will change.

7. Give the sort-block command, ^ KS.

8. On the top of the notepad window, the following instruction appears:

   Enter first column of sort key:

   Type 1 and press Return.

9. You are now requested to

   Enter last column of sort key:

   Type 2 and press Return. The six numbers are now arranged in ascending order.

10. If you want to print this marked block, turn on your printer and give the print command ^ KP.

You can sort lines of text alphabetically in the same way.

1. Clear the block markers by typing ^ KH.

2. Move to the top of the file with the command ^ PgUp.

3. Mark the beginning of a block with ^ KB.

4. Push the down-arrow four times.

5. Type ^ KK to mark the end of the block. The first four lines should change appearance.

6. Give the sort command ^ KS.

7. You will now see the following instruction on the screen:

   Enter first column of sort key:

   Answer with 1 and press Return.

8. Now you will see another request:

   Enter last column of sort key:

   Answer with 50 (the number of characters in the lines) and press Return. The four lines are now arranged in ascending alphabetical order (Figure 9.5).

9. Press ^ Alt to leave SideKick.

10. Press ^ Alt again to go directly to the notepad. Notice that the SideKick menu was bypassed this time because you previously left the notepad by pressing ^ Alt.

Saving Your Notepad File

As you can see, it is possible to leave the notepad with ^ Alt and then return to it with another ^ Alt without losing the current notepad

file. However, if you turn off your computer you will lose the file. Therefore if you want to save the text as a disk file, press F2. Leave the notepad again with ^Alt. (The bottom line identifies the F2 key with the
word *save* when the notepad is active.)

Adding the SideKick Command to AUTOEXEC.BAT

Now that you are familiar with the operation of the notepad, you
can use it to add commands to your AUTOEXEC.BAT file so SideKick
will always be loaded automatically. Let's see how:

1. Make the root directory current if you have a hard disk. For
a floppy system, put your system disk in drive A and make it
current.

2. Start the notepad with the ^Alt command.

3. The text from your previous work is still there. Press the F3 key
to indicate that you want to work on a new file. (If you have not
saved the previous work with the F2 key, SideKick will tell you
so and ask if you want to save it.) The previous file name still
shows on the top of the notepad window. However, it will disappear as soon as you begin typing the new file name.

Figure 9.5:   *Sorted lines in the notepad*

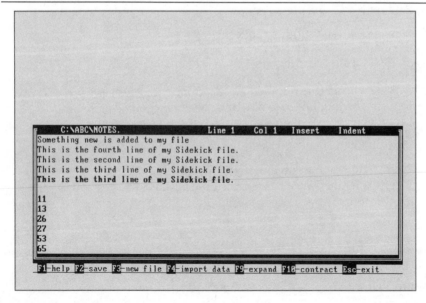

4. You can use wild cards to select your file name:

   A*.BAT

   A directory listing of all matching file names appears at the top of the screen.

5. Using the cursor-movement keys, move the cursor to the name AUTOEXEC.BAT and press Return. SideKick copies the file you want into the notepad so you can edit it. You do not have to type the complete name.

6. Move the cursor to the end of your AUTOEXEC.BAT file with the ^PgDn command.

7. If the cursor is at the end of the last line, ensure that the insert mode is on and press Return.

8. The cursor should be in column 1 on the line after the last line of the file. If you have a hard disk and have placed SideKick in subdirectory SK, write the lines:

   ```
   CD\SK
   SK
   CLS
   CD\
   ```

   If you have a floppy-disk system with RAM disk C, write the lines

   ```
   COPY  SK.HLP  C:>NUL
   C:
   A:SK
   A:
   ```

   For a floppy-disk system without a RAM disk, type

   ```
   SK
   ```

9. Press the F2 key to save the new version of your AUTOEXEC-.BAT file. The original version of the file is automatically re-named AUTOEXEC.BAK.

10. Leave SideKick by pressing ^Alt.

Now that you have added these commands to your AUTOEXEC.BAT file, Sidekick will automatically be loaded each time your computer is turned on or reset.

Importing, Cutting, and Pasting

Besides allowing you to create and alter a disk file, the SideKick notepad can capture any information on your video screen and make it a part of the disk file that you are editing with the notepad. It does not matter if the information is the output from a program, the listing of a file, or the text in the program that was running when SideKick was activated. In fact, it can even be information from other parts of SideKick such as the calendar or calculator. The SideKick manual calls the movement of text from the screen into the notepad file *importing* or *cutting*. (The reverse process, copying text *from* the notepad to another portion of the screen, is called *pasting*. We will consider pasting shortly.) You can import anything that appears on your screen. Let's say you want to import a part of your directory listing:

1. At the DOS prompt, type

   DIR

2. Press ^ Alt to pop up SideKick.

3. If the menu appears, press N to start the notepad.

4. Press F3 to clear the previous notepad file. You will be asked for a new file name. Type

   SKDIR

   for SideKick directory.

5. Press F4 to import text from the screen.

6. The notepad disappears and the original screen is visible. The cursor is in the upper-left corner. Move the cursor with the down-arrow key. Stop at the first file name in the directory listing.

7. Type the notepad symbol for the beginning of a block (^ KB).

8. Move the cursor down five lines with the down-arrow key. A marked block grows down column 1 as you move the cursor.

9. Move the cursor right until the growing block covers the right side of all five lines. You can move the cursor only with the four cursor keys for this operation. Moreover, if you hold down one of the cursor keys, it will repeat. Also note that you cannot use the Ctrl key with the cursor keys, nor can you use the Home, End, PgUp, or PgDn keys.

10. When the marked block includes all the text you want, press Esc. The notepad returns to the screen.

11. At this time you have no text in the notepad. But if you did, you could move the cursor to the position in your text where you wanted the marked block to go. For now, press the copy command, ^KC, and a copy of the marked block appears in the notepad at the cursor position. Of course the original text is still present on the screen underneath the notepad because this command only made a copy of it, it didn't delete it.

After you import a block of text from the screen to the notepad, you can save the information as a separate disk file. Then you can edit this new file or incorporate it into another file such as a report or letter. Do not confuse this operation with the COPY command that copies disk files. The notepad import command started with information on the video screen that was not part of a file.

It is also possible to transfer a block of text from the notepad into another program. Of course, the program that is to receive the text must be running and it must be expecting text to be typed at the keyboard. For example, you could be writing a report with WordStar or EDLIN (although you won't want to use EDLIN after you learn how to use Side-Kick's notepad).

Moving information from the notepad to another program is called *pasting*. When the two steps—importing text to the notepad and transferring information from the notepad to another program—are combined, the operation is called *cutting and pasting*. To paste text from the notepad to another program, mark the block of text in the notepad. As before, the beginning is marked with ^KB and the end is marked with ^KK. The marked block changes appearance.

Give the command ^KE; SideKick responds with the message

Press key to paste with:

The manual recommends Alt-F10, but you can use whatever combination you like. Just be careful not to use only a regular letter or number key or you won't be able to use that key for any other purpose until you clear it with ^KE Del. SideKick then asks

Block or Line:

Because you have highlighted a block, select Block. Leave SideKick with ^Alt and return to your application program. Now whenever you type the paste key you selected, it will reproduce the paste block. Press the paste key and the block of text from the notepad will appear in the file your program is working on. This paste key continues to be defined until you give the ^ KE Del command in the notepad.

You have learned how to give the most important notepad commands. There are many additional notepad commands that you will learn as you become more familiar with SideKick. Fortunately, it is not necessary to learn them all at the beginning. The commands are identified on two pages of the SideKick manual and also inside the back cover of the manual. You can also press the F1 key for a brief summary at any time you are working with your notepad.

The SideKick notepad can be used as an editor to create programs or other short text files. Its features are much better than those of EDLIN. However, SideKick cannot take the place of a word processor such as WordStar because it does not have word-processing features such as justification, subscripting, and boldfacing.

USING THE CALCULATOR

The SideKick calculator is similar to a real calculator. You can do addition, subtraction, multiplication, and division with it. Let's try it out:

1. Pop up the SideKick menu by typing ^ Alt.
2. Press the Alt-C keys to pop up the calculator. A graphic representation of a pocket calculator appears on the upper-right corner of the screen. However, the original text still shows. The bottom line of the screen identifies several keys and shows that the NumLock key is on. Thus you can use either the number pad keys or the regular number keys for the calculations.
3. If you like, you can use the calculator while you are working with another SideKick feature. Press Alt-N to pop up the notepad over part of the calculator. Suppose while you are writing a memo with the notepad, you need to know the number of days in four years. You want the value of 365 times 4 plus 1.
4. Press Alt-C to pop up the calculator over the notepad.
5. Press the keys

   3 6 5

   (the number of days in a year).

6. Press the * key (for multiplication).

7. Press the 4 key (for four years).

8. Press the plus key and the 1 key (to add the extra day for leap year).

9. Press the Return key to see the result. The number 1461.0000 appears at the top of the calculator (Figure 9.6).

10. Press

Alt-N

and the notepad pops over the calculator, covering the bottom part. However, the top of the calculator still shows the result. Therefore, you can now write the value onto your notepad.

There are other ways to get a value from the calculator to the notepad. For example, you can import it with the F4 key.

1. While in the notepad, press F4 and it disappears.

2. Move the cursor to the beginning of the number in the calculator window.

Figure 9.6: *SideKick calculator with notepad*

3. Press ^KB.

4. Press the right arrow to enlarge the block to the end of the number.

5. Press Esc. You are now back in the notepad.

6. Give the ^KC command and the number from the calculator appears in the notepad.

The previous method only works with the notepad. However, you might want to copy the calculator result into another program such as 1-2-3 or WordStar. Then you can use the calculator paste method. In this example, we will paste the result into the notepad. However, the method is general and you can use it for any other program.

1. Put the calculator window on top with the Alt-C command.

2. When the result you want is in the calculator answer window, press the P (for paste) key.

3. The message

   press key to paste with

   appears on the bottom line of the screen. Type Alt-P. *Do not press a regular key at this point or you will not be able to use it until you clear the calculator.*

4. Press Alt-N to put the notepad on top. (If you were working with another program such as WordStar or 1-2-3 you would press Esc or ^Alt to leave the calculator and return to your work.)

5. Press the Alt-P key and your calculated result appears in the notepad or whatever program you have running. You can press this key as many times as you want. Each time you do, the result is displayed.

   When you use the calculator you can see still most of the underlying text displayed by your editor. However, the calculator covers the right edge of the screen. If you need to see information that is covered by the calculator, you can move it somewhere else on the screen in this way:

1. Press the NumLock key and watch the NumLock indicator on the bottom line disappear.

2. Press the ScrollLock key and see the ScrollLock indicator turn on.

3. Use the four arrow keys to move the calculator to any convenient place on the screen.

4. Before you can use the calculator again you must press the NumLock and ScrollLock keys.

USING THE CALENDAR

Another feature of SideKick is the calendar. Let's try it out:

1. If the notepad or other part of SideKick is active, press Alt-L. Otherwise start SideKick with ^Alt and press the L key to pop up the calendar. (The letter C is used as a mnemonic for the calculator, so the third letter of word calendar is used for the calendar mnemonic.)

    The calendar for the current month is displayed on the left side of the screen (Figure 9.7); today's date is given at the top. Notice that the bottom line of the screen does not show the words NumLock or ScrollLock. Therefore, these keys are both off.

2. Press the left-arrow key to view the calendar for last month.

Figure 9.7: *SideKick calendar with calculator and notepad*

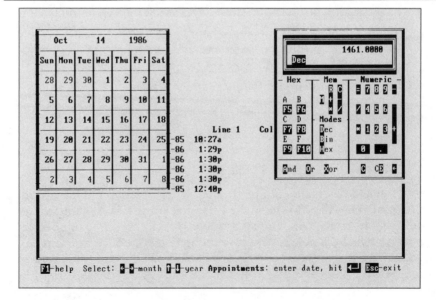

3. Press the right-arrow key twice to see the calendar for next month.

4. Press the left-arrow key to return to the current month.

5. Press the up-arrow key to see the calendar for next year.

6. Press the down-arrow key twice to see the calendar for last year.

7. Press the up-arrow key to return to the current calendar.

8. Press the Return key and an appointment sheet pops up on top of the calendar.

9. Press the ScrollLock key (the word ScrollLock will be identified on the bottom line) so that you can move the appointment sheet.

10. Move the appointments sheet off the calendar by pressing the right-arrow key.

11. Press the ScrollLock key a second time when the appointments sheet has cleared the calendar.

The appointments sheet shows the default file name—APPOINT.APP—but you can change the name to something else. Today's date is given at the top of the appointments sheet too. Down the left side are appointment times starting at 8 a.m. You can make notes for each half-hour period until 8:30 p.m.

12. Press the left- and right-arrow keys to view the appointments for yesterday and tomorrow.

13. If you fill up your appointments sheet and want a printout of it, press the F2 key.

14. Press Esc to remove the appointments sheet.

15. Press Esc again to remove the calendar.

VIEWING THE ASCII TABLE

Yet another feature of SideKick is the ASCII table. You learned in Chapter 6 that what you see on the video screen are ASCII characters. If you want to create boxes or other shapes on the screen, you need to refer to the ASCII table to find the appropriate symbols. For example, you can see that the four corners of a double-wall box have ASCII values of 201, 187, 200, and 188. You can view the ASCII characters with

SideKick (see Appendix C for a complete ASCII table):

1. If the notepad or other part of SideKick is active, press Alt-A (for ASCII). Otherwise start SideKick with ^ Alt and then press the A key to pop up the first part of the ASCII table. You will see the first 16 ASCII characters along with their decimal and hexadecimal values, the graphics equivalent (how the ASCII character appears on your screen), and the corresponding control character (for example, ^ A, ^ B).

2. Press the down-arrow key to see the second 16 characters.

3. Press the down-arrow key a second time and you will see 32 characters in the window, beginning with character number 32. This is the beginning of the printable ASCII characters, the letters, numbers, and special symbols. These characters are identified with the corresponding decimal and hexadecimal values.

4. Press Esc to remove the ASCII table.

HOW TO DEFINE YOUR KEYS WITH SUPERKEY

SuperKey is a resident utility that is designed to work with SideKick. Using SuperKey you can change the meaning of your keyboard keys. For example, on some keyboards, the Backslash key is just to the left of the Z key and the Shift key is just to the left of the Backslash key. You can program SuperKey to interchange the Shift and Backslash keys to make it easier to reach the Shift key. Sometimes the Esc key is on the left side of the keyboard and sometimes it is on the right. With SuperKey you can put it wherever you want.

With SuperKey you can also define Alt-T to write the current time on the screen and Alt-D to write the current date. You can define other Alt combinations to write your company name, or your city, state, and zip code.

You have learned that the F3 key can repeat the previous command. However, SuperKey keeps track of dozens of your previous commands. If you want to retrieve a command you gave earlier in the day, SuperKey can bring it back. Of course, you can edit any of the previous commands before running them again.

SuperKey will turn off your video screen if you are not using the keyboard so the information will not be permanently burned into the screen. After your screen has been turned off, SuperKey restores it to its previous forms as soon as you touch any key. The keyboard buffer can hold up to 15 characters you type while the computer is busy doing something else. If you type more than that, a beep tells you to wait. However, SuperKey can hold as many as 128 characters at a time. Therefore, you will never type ahead of the computer when SuperKey is present.

SuperKey must be installed just before SideKick. Therefore, if SideKick is already in place, you can remove it as described previously in this chapter. Then run SuperKey and SideKick again.

SuperKey must be purchased separately. You get both a manual and a disk. The 200-page manual describes how to redefine your keyboard. It also tells how to get SideKick and SuperKey to work together.

SUMMARY

In this chapter you learned how to install and use a resident utility called SideKick. You learned how to use the SideKick notepad to create and alter short files. You also saw how to use the calculator and calendar. You learned about the utility SuperKey, which can change the meaning of your keyboard and keep track of all your previous commands.

10 DOS Command and Program Summary

This chapter provides a quick reference guide to the DOS commands and programs, including some that are not described elsewhere in this book. The commands are arranged in alphabetical order and information is organized into consistent categories within each section for easy reference.

Each command is introduced by a brief statement describing its purpose. It is then identified as a built-in command or a program. Next, the format of the command is presented through examples. Note that when a file-name parameter is shown in the form PNAME, you must give only the primary part of the file name; you do not include the extension. When a parameter is given in the form PNAME.EXT, then you must enter both the primary name and the extension. When a parameter refers to a file on the default drive, you need not append the drive name to the file name. However, when the file is not on the default drive, you must include the drive name with the file name unless you have defined the location in a PATH command. The symbol D: by itself means that you are to enter only the drive name followed by a colon. The expression *ambig* means you can include the ? and *
ambiguous symbols in the file name to reference more than one file.

Following the format section is a description of the command. Some commands also include a brief section on use or give a text reference for further information.

Remember that this chapter is for quick reference. If you need a more detailed explanation of a command, turn to the chapter in the text where it is discussed or to your DOS manual for those commands that are not covered in this book.

ASSIGN

Changes name of disk drive
(ASSIGN.COM program)

Format

```
ASSIGN  A = C
ASSIGN  A = C;  B = C
ASSIGN
```

Description

Some applications programs can only be run on a particular drive, say A. But with the ASSIGN command you can run them on another drive such as a hard disk or RAM disk. The first form converts a request for drive A over to drive C. Some programs ignore this reassignment however. You must use the second form if you want to reassign two disks at once. You cannot make two assignments with two separate commands because each ASSIGN statement cancels the previous one. The second form converts requests for both drive A and drive B to drive C. The third form returns the assignment to its normal state.

ATTRIB

Changes read-only attribute of disk file
(ATTRIB.EXE program)

Format

```
ATTRIB  +R ambig
ATTRIB  -R ambig
ATTRIB  +A ambig
ATTRIB  -A ambig
ATTRIB  +A  +R ambigs
ATTRIB  ambig
```

Description

Each disk file can be marked as read-only so that it cannot be accidentally deleted. Once it is marked this way, the read-only *attribute* is *set*.

This file attribute is stored in the disk directory for the file. It is necessary to remove or *clear* the read-only attribute if you want to erase or alter a file. The read-only attribute can be set or cleared with the ATTRIB program. In addition, the current state of the attribute can be determined with this program.

A file that is marked as read-only appears in the directory display as usual. However, if you attempt to delete such a file with the DEL or ERASE command, DOS does not carry out the command. Rather, it displays the message

Access denied

Normally, you can replace one version of a file with a new version by copying the new version directly onto the older one. For example, if you have a file named WORK.COM on the current disk and give the command

COPY A:WORK.COM

DOS will delete the original version and copy the new version onto the current disk. However, if the original file is write protected, you will get the error message

Access denied

as with the DEL command.

Another file attribute, the *archive* attribute, shows whether a file has been changed since the last backup was made. The XCOPY program can make a backup copy of your files, then reset the archive attribute. Thus, if a file has not been changed since the last backup was made, it will not be copied again. While it is not normally necessary, the ATTRIB program can change the state of the archive attribute. It can also display the current state.

Use

To write protect a file, give the command

ATTRIB +R WORK.COM

where the first parameter (+ R) is a switch and the second parameter is the file name. You can protect a group of files by using wild cards. For example, the command

    ATTRIB +R *.COM

protects all COM files.

To remove write protection, use the –R switch. For example, the command

    ATTRIB –R *.COM

removes write protection for all COM files.

If you have DOS version 3.2 or later, you can set the archive attribute for a group of files with the command

    ATTRIB +A *.COM

and you can reset the archive attribute with the command

    ATTRIB –A *.COM

Both attributes can be changed with one command. However, there must be spaces on both sides of each switch:

    ATTRIB +A +R ambig

The current state of the write-protection attribute can be determined by omitting the switch. Thus, the command

    ATTRIB *.COM

displays all files that match the wild-card name. In addition, the letter R appears if the read-only attribute is set and the letter A appears if the archive attribute is set. Both letters appear if both attributes are set.

Normally, the ATTRIB command looks only in the current directory. However, you can add the /S switch to search the subdirectories too.

AUTOEXEC

Executes a series of commands to configure DOS to your specifications
(AUTOEXEC.BAT program)

Format

(Automatic execution on startup and reset)

Description

With this program you can give commands that DOS will read automatically every time it starts up. That way, you can configure DOS the way you want it. For more information, see Chapter 5.

BREAK

Allows program termination if you type ^ Break
(Built-in command)

Format

```
BREAK ON
BREAK = ON
BREAK
```

Description

You can prematurely terminate a running program if the BREAK feature is turned on. However, each time DOS is started, BREAK is automatically turned off. You can turn BREAK on with the first command. You can also turn it on automatically by placing the first form in the AUTOEXEC.BAT file or the second form in the CONFIG.SYS file. The third form displays the current state of the feature.

CD (OR CHDIR)

Changes the subdirectory on a hard disk
(Built-in command)

Format

```
CD\
CD\EDIT
CD SPELL
CD..
CD
```

Description

The first form of this command makes the root directory current and the second changes first to the root directory and then to the EDIT subdirectory. The third form checks the current directory for the subdirectory named SPELL and makes SPELL current (if it exists). The fourth version moves one level towards the root directory. The last version displays the current directory name and its path.

CHKDSK

Analyzes and summarizes the state of a disk
(CHKDSK.COM program)

Format

```
CHKDSK C:
CHKDSK C:/F
CHKDSK C:/V
CHKDSK PNAME.EXT
```

Description

This program checks the integrity of the disk surface. The second form recovers regions of the disk that are not usable and assigns them file names of the type FILE0001.CHK. You can then delete all the unusable regions with the command

```
DEL FILE*.CHK
```

The third form displays all files including hidden files in all subdirectories. It can be combined with the FIND program to locate a particular file. See Chapter 7 for more information.

A file name given as a parameter (the fourth example) is checked for fragmentation. The expression:

```
Contains 2 non-contiguous blocks
```

or

```
All specified file(s) are contiguous
```

is displayed.

CLS

Clears the video screen
(Built-in command)

Format

CLS

Description

Use this command when you want to clear the video screen. It can also turn color back on after a program has turned it off.

COMMAND

Processes keyboard commands
(COMMAND.COM program)

Format

(Automatic execution)

Description

DOS copies this program into memory each time the computer is started or reset and after certain programs have been run. As its name suggests, COMMAND reads your keyboard for a command and then carries out the request. For example, if you give the command

```
WS MYFILE
```

COMMAND tells the processor to copy the WordStar program into memory and start it up. It also tells WordStar that you included the parameter MYFILE.

When an executing program has finished, it returns control to COMMAND, which monitors the keyboard again for your input. However, the keyboard processor is not needed after it gives control to another program. Therefore, to gain more memory space, some programs destroy a part of COMMAND when they run. Then COMMAND must be loaded again from disk when the program finishes. DOS tries to

---

read COMMAND from the disk you started DOS from. This is generally A for a floppy system and C for a hard-disk system. Thus, COMMAND must be available at the end of a task.

DOS can find COMMAND if you start from a hard disk. However, with a floppy system, you may have changed disks. If COMMAND cannot be found, the error message

```
Insert disk with \command.com in drive A
and strike any key when ready
```

appears on your screen and DOS waits for your response. Place a disk containing COMMAND.COM in the requested drive and press the Return key. To change the way DOS looks for COMMAND, read Chapter 5.

COMP

Compares two disk files
(COMP.COM program)

Format

```
COMP ambig1 ambig2
COMP A: B:
COMP
```

Description

This command compares one or more sets of disk files with each other. If it finds differences, it displays them on the screen. The second form compares all files on both disks. If the file-name parameters are omitted, as in the third form, the program asks for them.

CONFIG.SYS

Configures DOS on startup
(CONFIG.SYS program)

Format

(Executes automatically on startup)

Description

This is a program you should create. It tells DOS to select the features you want, overriding the default values. If you provide this program, it is read each time DOS is started or restarted. See Chapter 5 for items to include. See also the SET command in this chapter.

COPY

Copies files
(Built-in command)

Format

```
COPY PNAME1.EXT PNAME2.EXT
COPY D:ambig
COPY ambig1 D:
COPY PNAME1.EXT + PNAME2.EXT PNAME3.EXT
COPY PNAME.EXT PRN
COPY CON PNAME.EXT
```

Description

This command duplicates one or more files, concatenates files, and transfers files to or from peripherals. The first form creates PNAME2.EXT by making a copy of PNAME1.EXT. The second form copies files from drive D to the current drive. The third form reverses the direction, copying files from the current drive to D. The fourth form concatenates the first two files into the third. The fifth form sends a file to the printer. The sixth form creates a disk file from information entered from the keyboard. Chapter 8 is devoted entirely to the COPY command.

DATE

Displays and sets date
(Built-in command)

Format

```
DATE
DATE 6-9-87
```

Description

If this command is given without a parameter, the current date is displayed in the following form:

Current date is Thu 9-11-1986

Then you are asked to enter a new date. Simply press the Return key if you do not want to change the date. Otherwise give the date as month, day, and year separated by hyphens. You don't have to type leading zeros for months and days less than 10. Although the program displays the day of the week (Thu in this example), you must not give the day when changing the date. The second form gives the new date as a parameter.

Unless you have DOS version 3.3, this command only changes the system clock. It does not change your battery-powered clock. Thus, if you change the date with this command, it will revert to the original value the next time you start your computer. You must run a special program to change the battery-powered clock.

DEL (OR ERASE)

Deletes disk files
(Built-in command)

Format

DEL PNAME.EXT
DEL *ambig*

Description

This command erases files that match the file name. (Write-protected files cannot be erased.) The wild-card symbols, ? and *, may be included. However, when you give the parameter *.*, DOS requests verification. If no file matches the given parameter, the error message

File not found

is displayed.

First give the corresponding command

DIR *ambig*

to get a list of the files that match the parameter. Then type DEL and press the F3 key to delete these files.

DIR

Displays a list of file names in the disk directory
(Built-in command)

Format

```
DIR
DIR D:
DIR FNAME.EXT
DIR ambig
DIR /P
DIR /W
```

Description

This command displays one or more file names from the disk directory. The file size and creation date are also given. If no parameter is given or if only a disk name is given, all file names in the directory are displayed. If there are more than 20 files, the list scrolls off the screen. You can give the /P (for page) switch so the display will stop when the screen has filled. Press any key to continue. The /W (for wide) switch displays five names on each line and the size and date are omitted.

DISKCOMP

Compares two floppy disks
(DISKCOMP.COM program)

Format

```
DISKCOMP A: B:
DISKCOMP A: A:
```

Description

This program compares two floppy disks to see if they are the same. The first form compares the disks in drives A and B. Use the second form if you have only one drive.

DISKCOPY

Duplicates a complete floppy disk
(DISKCOPY.COM program)

Format

```
DISKCOPY A: B:
DISKCOPY A: A:
```

Description

This program duplicates an entire floppy disk and formats it if necessary. The first form copies the contents of the disk in drive A to a disk in drive B. The second form uses only drive A. The program tells you when to change disks. If you have only one floppy drive, this is the best disk-copying method to use. However, in general it is not a good method for duplicating disks because it preserves the often-inefficient ordering of data. Use the FORMAT and COPY programs instead. Some commercial disks are copy protected. Then, DISKCOPY cannot complete the copy, or it will make a copy that does not work.

DRIVER

Establish logical drives
(DRIVER.SYS program)

Format

```
DEVICE = DRIVER.SYS /D:0/F:1
DEVICE = DRIVER.SYS /D:1/T:80/N:9
```

Description

This program establishes additional logical drives for any disk drive. Then you can address that drive with more than one letter.

The /D switch designates which drive is to be replicated. The values 0 and 1 replicate the A and B drives respectively. For example, suppose you have one 5-inch and one 3.5-inch drive, addressed as A and B respectively. In addition, you have a hard disk addressed as C. Then, if you place the commands

```
DEVICE = DRIVER.SYS /D:0/F:0
DEVICE = DRIVER.SYS /D:1/F:1
```

in the CONFIG.SYS file, the 5-inch drive (D:0) will also be drive D and the 3.5-inch drive (D:1) will also be drive E. Then you can more easily duplicate files and complete disks.

Use

You cannot run this program yourself. Instead, you place the command into the CONFIG.SYS file. The /F switch is a form factor, describing the properties of the drive. You can also specify the number of tracks and the number of sectors per track with the /T and /N switches, respectively. The form factor is defined as follows:

Form F	Size inches	Bytes	Tracks T	Sectors/track N
0	5.25	360K	40	9
1	5.25	1.2M	80	15
2	3.5	720K	80	9
7	3.5	1.4K	80	18

EDLIN

Creates and alters a text file
(EDLIN.COM program)

Format

```
EDLIN
EDLIN PNAME.EXT
EDLIN PNAME.EXT D:
```

Description

The EDLIN program is a simple line-oriented text editor. With it you can create and alter text files used for computer programs, letters, and reports. It does not include a video screen mode, nor does it provide word processing features such as justification, subscripting, and boldfacing.

Use

The operation of EDLIN is described in detail in Chapter 4. A brief summary of the commands is given here. In the following list, n, x, and y specify line numbers. If a line number is omitted, the current line number is used. The # symbol means a large number.

Command	Explanation
nA	Copies (appends) n lines from the original file to the end of the text in memory.
x,y,zC	Copies lines x–y to line z.
x,yD	Deletes lines x–y.
E	Ends the edit session normally and saves the file to disk.
nI	Inserts text in front of line n. Press ^ Break to terminate the command.
x,yL	Lists lines x–y. Current line does not move.
x,y,nM	Moves lines x–y to line n.
x,yP	Displays lines x–y and makes the last line of the display current. Make x equal to y to change current line to x.
Q	Quits editing session, discarding all changes. The original file is intact.
x,yRoldtext ^ Znewtext	Replaces *oldtext* with *newtext* through lines x–y.
x,ySstring	Finds the next occurrence of the given string between lines x–y.
nTPNAME .EXT	Reads the file PNAME.EXT into memory at line n.
nW	Copies (writes) n lines from memory to the new file and deletes the corresponding lines from memory (not needed when the session is ended with the E command).

n   Allows you to change line n using the function keys and the Del, Ins, and Backspace keys. However, you can make changes more easily with the R command.

ERASE

(See DEL)

FASTOPEN

Starts programs quicker
(FASTOPEN.EXE program)

Format

```
FASTOPEN C:
FASTOPEN C: = 50
```

Description

Each time you run a program, DOS must search the disk directory to find the name of the program you want to run. Since programs are not placed into the directory in any order, it may take a noticeable time to locate a program so it can be started. However, after you run FAST-OPEN, it keeps a log of each program you have run. Then, if you run a program a second time, DOS checks the FASTOPEN list first. By this means, you can greatly speed the startup of frequently used programs.

With the first form, FASTOPEN keeps track of as many as 35 programs. If you want FASTOPEN to watch a different number, use the second form. You can specify a number from 10 to 999.

FDISK

Prepares a new hard disk
(FDISK.EXE program)

Format

```
FDISK
```

Description

A new hard disk is not usable until the surface has been partitioned and then formatted. FDISK does the partitioning. Then use FORMAT for the formatting. You only have to run this program once. Version 3.3 can partition a disk larger than 32M bytes into two or more disks. See Chapter 5 for details.

FIND

Searches for a pattern of letters in text
(FIND.EXE program)

Format

FIND "string" PNAME.EXT

Description

This program looks in the file PNAME.EXT for the characters in "string". If found, the file name and line containing the string are displayed. The character *string* must be enclosed in quotation marks. When this command is combined with others using a fence, it is possible to perform a sequence of complicated operations. See Chapter 7 for more information.

FORMAT

Prepares a new disk
(FORMAT.COM program)

Format

FORMAT B:/S/V
FORMAT B:/V
FORMAT B:/V/T:80/N:9

Description

A new disk, including a hard disk, must be prepared before it is used for the first time. This step is called formatting. It also may be necessary to format a disk if the power fails when the computer is writing information. The format program destroys any information on the disk surface. Be careful not to accidentally format a working disk.

The /S switch places three DOS files onto the disk. You must give this switch when formatting a hard disk or a system disk. However, the DOS files are not needed on other disks and unnecessarily take up space. Therefore, do not give the /S switch for data disks.

When the /V (for volume name) switch is given, the program asks for a disk name. Choose a name that will remind you of the subject matter that will be placed on the disk. The name may contain as many as 11 letters, numbers, and blanks. See the LABEL command.

With version 3.3, you can specify the number of tracks with /T and the number of sectors per track with /N. This is useful for creating low-density disks in a high-density drive.

LABEL

Changes the name of a disk
(LABEL.COM program)

Format

```
LABEL B:RECEIPTS
LABEL B:
```

Description

Floppy disks can be easily mixed up. Therefore, you should assign a name to each one that suggests the nature of the information that is to be stored. You can assign a name when the disk is formatted. However, you can also assign or change the name at any time using the LABEL program. The name may contain as many as 11 letters, numbers, and blanks. (This command is not included in DOS 2.)

MD (OR MKDIR)

Creates a subdirectory on a hard disk
(Built-in command)

Format

```
MD\EDIT
```

Description

This command creates a new subdirectory on the hard disk. It is usually best to have only a single level of subdirectories all attached to the root directory. That is, to avoid confusion, there should not be subdirectories of subdirectories. Then, give the command

    CD\

to ensure that the root directory is current before giving the MD command. If a subdirectory is current, this command will make the new directory a subdirectory of the current subdirectory. On the other hand, if you first give the command

    MD\EDIT

from a subdirectory, DOS changes to the root directory and makes the new directory a subdirectory of the root directory. Type C and press the F3 key to issue the command

    CD\EDIT

to make the new subdirectory the current one.

MODE

Configures video screen and serial port
(MODE.COM program)

Format

    MODE COM1:2400,N,8,1,P
    MODE LPT1:=COM1
    MODE LPT1
    MODE N

Description

The standard printer is a dot-matrix device that connects to the parallel port named LPT1. DOS is designed to run the printer from this port. However, most daisy-wheel and laser printers are designed to run from the serial port named COM1. If you have one of these, you must give two commands: first type

    MODE COM1:2400,N,8,1,P

to set the serial port to match the requirements of your printer (2400 speed in this example). Then type

    MODE LPT1: = COM1

which tells DOS to send printer output to the serial port rather than the usual parallel port. Put these two commands into a batch file named SERIAL.BAT. Then when you give the command

    SERIAL

you can use your daisy-wheel printer.

   You can have two printers attached to your computer at the same time. For example, you can have a dot-matrix printer connected to the parallel port and a daisy-wheel printer connected to the serial port. Then you can switch to the daisy-wheel printer with the previous command. Return to the dot-matrix printer with the command

    MODE LPT1

   The MODE command is also used to change the video-screen mode for the graphics screen or to switch between screens if you have both the monochrome and the color-graphics screens. Give the command

    MODE *N*

where N can have the following values:

40	for a graphics screen 40 characters wide
80	for a graphics screen 80 characters wide
BW40	for graphics no color, width 40
BW80	for graphics no color, width 80
CO40	for graphics color, width 40
CO80	for graphics color, width 80
MONO	for a change to monochrome

   Three types of video screens are available: monochrome, graphics, and extended graphics. The graphics screen is usually color.

However, it is also possible to use a black-and-white video screen instead and display graphics without color. (You can distinguish the black-and-white graphics screen from the monochrome screen by the resolution of the text. Letters and numbers displayed on the graphics screen are very difficult to read.)

Color mode is the default for the graphics screen. However, when a program sends color information to a black-and-white screen, it may be impossible to read. The black-and-white rendition of red letters on a blue screen is a uniform gray. Thus, if you have a black-and-white graphics screen, you should set the mode to black-and-white graphics. That is, you should turn off color mode. Then it will be easier to read the screen. To do so, type

    MODE BW80

Put this command into your AUTOEXEC.BAT file so color mode for graphics will always be off.

MORE

Stops scrolling when video screen is filled
(MORE.COM program)

Format

    ┆ MORE
    MORE <SAMPLE.TXT

Description

This is a filter program that alters the behavior of other programs that display information on the screen. For example, if you display a large file on the video screen with the command

    TYPE SAMPLE.TXT

the text will scroll off the screen unless you stop the scrolling with the ^ S command. However, it is difficult to stop the screen at a particular place. By contrast, consider the command

    TYPE SAMPLE.TXT ┆ MORE

The fence (¦) is placed between two commands. Now, the output from TYPE is not displayed directly on the video screen, but is sent to the MORE filter. MORE displays only 23 lines on the screen at a time and on the bottom of the screen it displays the following message:

　　– more –

When you have read the information on the screen, press the space bar to see the next screen. The command:

　　MORE <SAMPLE.TXT

does the same thing, but is shorter.
　　The triple command

　　DIR ¦ SORT ¦ MORE

sorts the directory listing and stops each time the screen is filled.

PATH

　　Establishes search path for program execution
　　(Built-in command)

Format
　　PATH C:\DOS
　　PATH D:\;C:\DOS
　　PATH
　　PATH;

Description
　　A hard disk is partitioned into subdirectories to make it more manageable. However, this partitioning is both an advantage and a disadvantage. When there are many files in each directory and you want to run a program, you must first find the directory it is located in. Therefore, it is best to keep all executable programs in one or two subdirectories. You can use the PATH command to tell DOS which directory has your executable program. Then you can run your programs from any subdirectory or from any disk without having to specify a directory.

The command:

    PATH C:\DOS

tells DOS that all your programs are stored in the subdirectory DOS on disk C. Then if you want to create a file named PAYROLL while subdirectory WORK is current, give the command

    EDLIN PAYROLL

and EDLIN will be run from subdirectory DOS even though that subdirectory is not current. The PATH command directs DOS to the program given in the command (EDLIN in this example) but it does not locate the parameter (PAYROLL, in this example). Therefore, the parameter is referenced to the current directory, or drive.

You can establish a path to more than one subdirectory. Separate each directory with a semicolon. For example, type the following command:

    PATH D:\;C:\DOS

This command tells DOS to first look on drive D and if the program cannot be found there, to look in the subdirectory DOS of drive C. However, you may find it counterproductive to include more than one or two directories in the search path, especially if you are not an expert typist. Let us see why. If you mean to type

    DIR

but instead type

    DUR

by mistake, DOS will search each directory listed in the PATH command looking for the program DUR. After DOS has searched all the directories and has not found the file, it gives the error message

    Bad command or file name

The more directories given in the PATH command, the longer it takes DOS to display the error message. Of course, if you notice a typing mistake, press ^ Break to interrupt the search.

For a floppy-disk system, give the command

    PATH A:\

Then keep drive B current but keep your programs on drive A. The command

    EDLIN SAMPLE.TXT

will then run EDLIN from drive A even when drive B is current.

If you use a RAM disk with a floppy-disk system, give the command:

    PATH C:\;A:\

Then DOS will first look on the RAM disk. Then, if a program cannot be found there, it will look on drive A.

You can determine the current search path by typing the command

    PATH

The response might be

    PATH = C:\DOS

or

    No path

if none has been established. If you always use the same search path, put the PATH command near the end of your AUTOEXEC.BAT file.

To remove the search path, type

    PATH;

PROMPT

Establishes command prompt
(Built-in command)

Format

    PROMPT PG
    PROMPT $P,$D$G

PROMPT
PROMPT $E[0;30;46m PG$E[1;37;44m

Description

The initial DOS prompt gives the current drive name and a > symbol. However, the prompt can be changed to something else. The first example creates a prompt that identifies the subdirectory name and the drive at all times. This is useful when you have a hard disk. The second example is like the first, but also displays the date. For example, the prompt might look like this:

C:\DOS,Thu 9-11-1986>

Notice that a comma appears in the prompt because a comma was given in the PROMPT command. The third example resets the prompt to the DOS default value.

The text on a color screen will be white letters on a field of black unless you change it. The fourth example makes a color screen more pleasing. Normal text will appear as white letters on a field of blue except for the prompt, which will be black letters on a field of aqua. Before you can use this prompt, you must place the command

DEVICE = ANSI.SYS

in your CONFIG.SYS file. The letter *m* that appears twice must be given in lowercase.

Any character included in the PROMPT parameter that does not follow a dollar sign ($) will appear in the prompt. However, characters following the dollar sign tell DOS to include specific elements in its prompt. The characters and their meanings are listed below:

$B	The ¦ character
$D	The date
$E	The Esc character
$G	The greater-than (>) character
$H	Backspace to hide previous character
$L	The less-than (<) character
$N	The current drive
$P	The current path
$Q	The equal sign (=)

$T	The time
$V	The DOS version
$$	The $ character
$_(underline)	Start new line

REN (OR RENAME)

Renames a disk file
(Built-in command)

Format

```
REN OLDNAME.EXT NEWNAME.EXT
REN ambig1 ambig2
```

Description

The RENAME command changes the name of a disk file. Only the name in the directory is changed; the file itself is not altered. The wild-card symbols, ? and *, may be used, but they should occur in identical positions in both names or only be used in one name. For example

```
REN FNAME?.EXT FNAME?.BAK
REN FNAME.EXT *.BAK
```

It is best to rename files only in the current directory. However, you can rename files in other directories by including the directory name with the first parameter.

RD (OR RMDIR)

Deletes subdirectory
(Built-in command)

Format

```
RD \SUBDIR
RD SUBDIR
```

Description

This command removes a subdirectory, but only after all files have been deleted with DEL. Some programs write a hidden file that cannot be deleted with DEL. Then the RD command will not work. The first example removes a directory that is a subdirectory of the root directory. The second example removes a directory that is a subdirectory of the current directory.

SET

Changes and displays current state of DOS features
(Built-in command)

Format

```
SET  COMSPEC = C:\COMMAND.COM
SET
SET  SPOOLER = 48K
```

Description

The first example tells DOS to look for COMMAND.COM on drive C. The second version displays the current state of COMSPEC, PATH, and PROMPT. For example, the response to SET might be the following:

```
COMSPEC = C:\COMMAND.COM
PATH = C:\DOS
PROMPT = $P$G
```

COMSPEC is changed with the SET command but the PATH and PROMPT commands are given separately.

You can define additional symbols with the third form. If this command is placed in the batch file that loads the spooler program, you can later determine its size by giving the SET command. The response will be:

```
SPOOLER = 48K
```

SORT

Sorts lines of a text file
(SORT.EXE program)

Format

```
SORT  <FILE1 >FILE2
DIR ¦ SORT /R / + 10 ¦ MORE
```

Description

The SORT filter arranges lines of a file in alphabetical or numeric order. Input to SORT can be a disk file (when the < symbol is used) or the output from another program (when the ¦ symbol is used). Output goes to the video screen, to a new disk file (when the > symbol is used) or to another program (when the ¦ symbol is used).

The /R switch reverses the order, from Z to A and 9 to 0. The sorting is normally based on the complete line starting at column one. However, the / + switch starts at the column number following the + symbol. For example, the command

DIR ¦ SORT / + 16

will sort the directory entries by file size because file size begins at the 16th column of the directory listing.

SUBST

Establishes a subdirectory as a separate disk
(SUBST.EXE program)

Format

SUBST D: C:\EDIT
SUBST D: /D

Description

With a hard disk, it is convenient to keep executable programs in one directory, say DOS, and auxiliary editing programs in a second directory, say EDIT. Then you can create and alter text in a third directory, say, PAYROLL. However, some older programs such as WordStar version 3 do not accept DOS path names. Therefore this technique will not work. The SUBST program provides a solution to this problem. Give the command

SUBST D: C:\EDIT

and DOS will treat all programs in subdirectory EDIT as if they were located on disk D. You can configure WordStar to look for its auxiliary files on drive D. Then, place the main WordStar program in your DOS subdirectory which is referenced in a PATH command. After that, you can access WordStar from any subdirectory just by typing its name

    WS SAMPLE.TXT

Undo the effect of SUBST with the second form. (SUBST is not included in DOS 2.)

SYS

Writes DOS system to disk
(SYS.COM program)

Format

    SYS
    SYS C:

Description

The FORMAT program places the two, hidden system files on a disk that is used to start up DOS. However, when a new version of DOS is available, you can upgrade without reformatting the disk. Boot the new version of DOS from a floppy disk in drive A. Then give the SYS command to copy the new version of DOS to your hard disk, or a floppy disk that already has a copy of DOS. You cannot use the SYS command to place the DOS files on a disk that was formatted without the /S switch. The command processor, COMMAND.COM must be separately transferred with the COPY command.

TIME

Displays and allows alteration of time
(Built-in command)

Format

    TIME
    TIME 13:7
    TIME 13.7 (version 3)

Description

This program displays the time and allows you to alter it. Enter the time as hour and month separated by colons. You can also add seconds if you want. Use the 24-hour clock; thus, 1 p.m. is 13. A leading zero may be omitted for values less than 10. Unless you have version 3.3, this command only changes the system clock. It does not change your battery-powered clock. If you change the time with this command, say from standard to daylight time, your system clock will revert to the original time when you start your computer again. Normally, you must run a special program to change the battery-powered clock. However, DOS version 3.3 will reset the battery-powered clock as well as the system clock. A period can be used instead of the colon to avoid using the Shift key (not in version 2).

TREE

Displays subdirectory paths
(TREE.COM program)

Format

```
TREE
TREE /F
```

Description

When there are many subdirectories and many more files on a hard disk, it is difficult to visualize where everything is and how to move from place to place. The TREE program is designed to show the organization of the disk. Unfortunately, this program does not give a good graphic picture of the subdirectory structure. Several commercial programs are available that do a better job. XTREE is a good one. It not only shows the directory structure and the files in each directory, but it also allows you to delete unwanted files.

TYPE

Displays a text file on the video screen
(Built-in command)

Format

```
TYPE PNAME.EXT
TYPE PNAME.EXT >PRN
TYPE PNAME.EXT ¦ MORE
```

Description

The TYPE command displays the contents of a text file on the video screen. The display can be stopped by pressing ˆS when the screen is filled. Press ˆS again to resume scrolling. A file can be printed using >PRN as in the second example. The third example automatically stops the scrolling when the screen is filled. Press any key to see the next screen. Be careful not to use TYPE to display COM or EXE files or the screen will fill with meaningless symbols.

VDISK

Establishes a RAM disk
(VDISK.SYS program)

Format

```
DEVICE = VDISK.SYS 256
DEVICE = VDISK.SYS 512 /E
```

Description

This system program establishes a RAM disk by reserving a portion of memory for it. It makes this portion of memory into a very fast disk. You cannot run the VDISK program yourself. Rather, you must place one of the above commands into the CONFIG.SYS file. The first form creates a RAM disk of 256K bytes with a portion of main memory. Of course, the usable memory is reduced accordingly. The second form is only for PC AT-type computers that have more than 640K bytes of memory. If you have extra memory, the regular memory is not reduced when you add a RAM disk.

VER

Displays DOS version
(Built-in command)

Format

VER

Description

There are several different versions of DOS. The major versions (each of which represents substantial revisions) are 1, 2, and 3. There are also minor versions (with minor changes) such as 2.0, 2.1, 3.0, 3.1, 3.2, and 3.3. Version 1 is so different that many newer programs cannot be run with it. Version 2 uses a hard disk inefficiently. Version 3.0 has bugs in it. Therefore, you should only use versions 3.1, 3.2, or 3.3. You can easily determine the version of DOS by giving the VER command. When you type VER, the response is something like:

MS-DOS Version 3.10

VERIFY

Verifies that a disk file is correctly written
(Built-in command)

Format

VERIFY ON
VERIFY = ON
VERIFY

Description

Information is stored magnetically on the surface of a disk. Occasionally, the information is incorrectly written to the disk. This can occur if the disk surface is damaged or if a flake of magnetic material momentarily sticks to the write head. The VERIFY command tells DOS to check each disk file it creates to see that it is correct magnetically. Unfortunately, the data in the file are not checked for errors.

Each time DOS is started or restarted, VERIFY is automatically turned off. You can turn VERIFY on with the first command shown above. However, you can also turn it on automatically by placing the first form in the AUTOEXEC.BAT file or the second form in the CONFIG.SYS file. If you type the third form, DOS displays the current state of this feature.

VOL

Displays disk name
(Built-in command)

Format

VOL
VOL A:

Description

Floppy disks can be easily mixed up because they look so much alike. To avoid mixing up your disks, you should assign them names when you format them and write those names on the label of the disk. Then when you print a listing of the directory it will identify the disk name, also called a volume label. (Put the listing in the disk envelope.)

The disk name can contain as many as 11 characters including spaces. If you type the VOL command, DOS will identify the label of the current disk, for example:

Volume in drive A is EDIT 3

or

Volume in drive A has no label

(if no label has been assigned).

XCOPY

Makes backup copies of files
(XCOPY.EXE program)

Format

XCOPY C:\DOS*.* /M
XCOPY C:\DOS*.* /A
XCOPY C:\DOS*.* /D:8-9-87
XCOPY C:\DOS*.* /P
XCOPY C:\DOS*.* /W
XCOPY A:*.* /S

Description

This program is similar to the COPY command. It can copy one or more files from one subdirectory to another. Unlike COPY, which only copies one file at a time, XCOPY copies as many files into memory as possible. Then it writes them to the target disk. Thus XCOPY can copy a group of files faster than COPY.

XCOPY is especially useful for making backup copies of your important files, because it can use the archive attribute. The *archive* attribute, discussed under the command ATTRIB, shows when a file has been created or altered but not backed up. Then, if you have DOS version 3.2 or newer, you can make a backup copy of your files using the XCOPY program. This program resets the archive attribute when making a backup copy. Then, the next time you make backup copies with XCOPY, only those files that were changed or created since the privious backup will be copied. This greatly reduces the time needed to backup a large disk.

Use

As with the COPY command, it is best to copy from another directory into the current one. Therefore, to backup the DOS subdirectory on drive C to the current floppy disk in drive A, give the command

    XCOPY C:\DOS*.* /M

The /M switch tells XCOPY to copy all files that have the archive attribute set, that is, that have been changed or added since the last backup. The first time you give this command, all files will be copied. But since XCOPY also resets the archive attribute at this time, these files will not be copied the next time you give this command.

If you want to make two backup copies, use the /A switch first. The command

    XCOPY C:\DOS*.* /A

is like the previous one. Only those files with the archive attribute set are copied. However, the attribute is not reset. Thus you make the first copy with the A switch and the second one with the M switch.

The /D switch is an interesting variation. The command

    XCOPY C:\DOS*.* /D:3-9-87

copies only those files that were created on or after the given date. Of course, you can combine switches. The command

    XCOPY C:\DOS*.* /A/D:3-9-87

copies only those files with the archive attribute set that were created on or after the given date.

An extra margin of safety is provided with the /P switch. Then you are asked for permission to copy each file. You must answer Y or N. The /W switch is used when you have only one floppy disk. Without the /W switch, XCOPY begins copying as soon as it is executed. However, when you add the /W switch, XCOPY waits for you to change disks before starting.

The /S switch copies files not only from the current directory but also from all subdirectories of the current directory. Furthermore, the corresponding subdirectories will be created on the target disk if they do not already exist. Suppose, for example, that you have made a backup floppy disk for the files on the root directory and the DOS and PROG subdirectories. Then, if you make the root directory of the hard disk current, you can restore these files to the hard disk with the command

    XCOPY A:*.* /S

The /S switch will create new DOS and PROG subdirectories if necessary and copy the files.

Hints for Beginners

Although your computer is a complex machine that must be treated with respect, if you follow some simple procedures and precautions you should be able to make the best use of your computer and avoid problems. This appendix presents two kinds of information: practical techniques for using and caring for your hardware and hints for doing the operations most effectively.

THE WORKSPACE

If you keep your computer workspace organized you will find it easier to use your computer and avoid problems. Make sure all necessary documentation, blank disks, computer programs, and other supplies are available. Make a list of the steps needed to start up your computer and then keep that list by the computer. Here is a typical list of supplies:

- Computer log
- System disk
- Disks for applications programs
- New floppy disks
- Printer paper
- Extra printwheel
- Printer ribbons
- Envelopes
- Computer manual
- This book
- Manuals for application programs

To create your computer log, buy a bound notebook. In it, keep a chronological record of procedures and hardware changes. Record the details needed to start up your computer. If you change the DOS version, note the date and version number. When you configure a program such as WordStar or Sidekick, record the features you selected. Also record the switch settings on the printer. If something peculiar happens, write down the details. Then you can describe the event to another person.

FLOPPY DISKS

Always treat your floppy disks carefully because they can be easily damaged. Floppy disks are magnetic media. Therefore, do not place them near a magnetic field or a steel object that might be magnetized. Magnetic fields can be produced by telephones, screwdrivers, steel desks, and any other steel objects. When traveling by air, do not place disks in your luggage. Hand-carry them and be sure to ask for a separate inspection when you board the plane. Do not let the disks be X-rayed, since the X-ray machine creates a magnetic field.

Always place disks in their envelopes when you are not using them. Do not expose them to dust or smoke. Be especially careful if you live in a dry climate because disks can accumulate a static charge that makes dust stick to the surface. Do not touch or clean the disk surface or open the outer cover.

You should always place a label on each disk. Write something on the label that will remind you of the contents. For example, choose descriptive names like MEMOS, QUART_REPT, or PHONE_LIST. Also, magnetically code the label on the disk with the LABEL program.

Never write on a 5-inch disk with a pen, pencil, or other sharp object because the pressure can damage the surface. Instead, use a felt-tipped pen or write on the label and then apply it to the disk. Use only the labels that are especially made for use on floppy disks. The wrong kind of label can damage the disk or the disk drive. Do not bend disks or expose them to heat or direct sunlight.

If your climate is dry, or you air-condition your computer room, you should try to control static electricity. Otherwise, sparks from your body can damage the computer. An antistatic spray can be used on carpeting.

DAMAGED FILES

A disk file can be damaged because of operator error, a system malfunction, or a power failure. If a program is damaged, you may not be able to run it. If a text file is damaged, it may not be possible to edit or list it. If you have a backup copy of a damaged file, delete the damaged version and make a new copy from the backup.

There are several commercial programs that you can use to recover damaged files. The Norton Utilities is a good one.

DAMAGE TO THE DISK SURFACE

The surface of a disk can be damaged in one of two ways. A region can be incorrectly magnetized, or there can be a defect such as a scratch in the surface. It may be possible to correct a magnetic fault with FORMAT. However, if the surface is damaged, the disk should be discarded. A hard disk can automatically find faulty areas and mark them as unusable.

THE PRINTER

A computer printer will work very reliably for months or even years without needing attention if it is treated with care. Switches on the printer must be correctly set for full or half duplex, online or local, single or double line feed, paper-out sensor, baud rate, parity, and word length. Read the manual for your printer so you can understand what these settings do and how to change them.

If your printer is slow, you may be tempted to walk away from the computer while it is printing. Be sure you check the operation often to see that everything is in order. This is especially important at the beginning of a listing, because the paper might jam in the printer. You should always be present when printing adhesive labels, since they are more likely to jam than regular paper.

Printer ribbons may be either carbon or cloth. All carbon ribbons and some cloth ribbons move in only one direction. However, some cloth ribbons occasionally reverse direction. At the moment of reversal the characters tend to be printed too lightly or not at all. Whenever a problem occurs during printing, the listing will have to be restarted. If the first part is all right, it may be possible to restart the listing at the place where the problem occurs. Word processors such as WordStar have provisions for this. On the other hand, if a file is short, it may be easier to restart the listing from the beginning.

If the printer does not work when the system is turned on, check all printer settings. In particular, check that the online/local switch is set to online. Also, check that the cord from the computer to the printer is in place. If you use two different printers with two versions of WordStar, be sure that you have the correct version.

DISK FILES

INITIAL PRECAUTIONS

Be sure to format a new disk before you use it for the first time. Always make a backup copy of any new program or disk before it is first used. Then put the original away in a safe place. During a long editing session, frequently save your work in case of power failure or human error. In addition, regularly make a backup copy on another disk.

Make a listing of the disk directory by engaging the printer with ^P and then giving the command

    DIR *.*

Place the listing in the disk sleeve. Then you can readily determine the contents. Keep a backup copy of important disks in a separate location so that you do not risk losing all your information at once. If you have an office computer, keep the backup disks at home. If you have a home computer, keep the backups at the office.

SIZE

There is a limit to how much information can be stored on each disk as well as to the available number of directory entries. As more and more files are saved on a disk, the free space can become exhausted. Another problem can arise if a single file is larger than the capacity of the disk. For fastest editing and duplication, file size should be limited to 40–50K bytes. For example, you can keep each chapter of a book as a separate file rather than making the entire book into one file. Of course, it is more difficult to divide a data file, such as a list of customer names, into several parts. One solution is to arrange the list in alphabetical order. Then you can break it into several parts—A–L and M–Z for example—in separate files.

Before you edit a file on a floppy disk, determine the file size and the remaining disk space with DIR. If you want the edited file to be placed on the same disk as the original, there must be sufficient room. In fact, the remaining space on the disk should be more than the size of the original file because the editor may need some working space. For example, if the file to be edited is 40K bytes long, the disk should contain at least 60K bytes of free space in addition to the original file. If there is not enough space, you can tell the editor to place the new version on a different disk from the original file.

Sorting large files can also be a problem. Some sorting programs use the disk for working space. Then you must have room on the disk for both the sorted file and the original file. Other sorting programs let you change to a new disk when it is time to save the sorted version. A sorting program, such as SuperSort by MicroPro, can sort very large files from disk to disk. We saw in Chapter 9 that SideKick can sort a text file. Also, the DOS program SORT was discussed in Chapters 3 and 10. See my book *Turbo BASIC Programs for Scientists and Engineers* (SYBEX 1987) for sorting routines.

SYSTEM FILES

Two hidden DOS files and the command processor, COMMAND-.COM, are located on your system disk. The hidden files are only needed when you first turn on your computer or when you reset it. The command processor is not only needed when you turn on or reset your computer but also after certain programs that erase part of the command processor have been run.

Since it is only necessary to have the hidden system files on the system disk, they unnecessarily take up space on other disks. On the other hand, the command processor, COMMAND.COM, should be on your system disk and also on those disks with programs that erase the command processor. However, this is not really a problem. If DOS needs to read the command processor, but cannot find it, the message

```
Not ready error reading drive A
Insert disk with \COMMAND.COM in drive A
and strike any key when ready
```

is displayed. Put your system disk in drive A and press Return. To prevent this from happening again, place the file COMMAND.COM on the disk you just ran.

In Chapter 5, you learned how to put COMMAND.COM on a RAM disk and tell DOS to find the command processor there.

EDITING

If you need to change a word or expression throughout the file, the substitution command of your editor can accomplish this conveniently (See Chapter 4 for details). You can also use the substitution command to save yourself some typing time and effort when a complicated expression is needed at many places in a report. Let us see how to do this.

Suppose, for example, that the chemical compound naphthalene is mentioned 30 times in a report. At each place, enter a symbol such as N$ instead. Then after the document is finished, use the substitution command to change each occurrence of N$ to naphthalene. Another way to enter long expressions is to program some of your keys with Superkey. See Chapter 9 for details.

EXECUTING A SEQUENCE OF COMMANDS

You can easily execute a lengthy sequence of commands or a frequently used set of commands by creating a disk file of the commands and giving it the file extension BAT. See Chapter 7 for more details.

PRINTING SEVERAL FILES AT ONCE

It is possible to print several files by using COPY with a wild-card file name or with concatenation (see Chapter 8). Alternatively, you can create a batch file, called PRINT.BAT for example, to print several files with one command.

ERASING A DISK

You can erase all the files on a disk if you no longer need them. Then you can use the disk for other files. Give the command

```
DEL *.*
```

Then you can change the volume name with the LABEL program. Of course, you can erase individual files by giving the DEL command and the file name.

TERMINATING EXECUTION

If you accidentally execute the wrong program or execute a program with the wrong parameters, it may be possible to terminate execution (that is, stop the program before it finishes) by typing ^BREAK. Be sure you have turned on the BREAK feature as described in Chapter 5. If you cannot terminate programs in this way, you can interrupt execution by pressing Ctrl, Alt, and Del simultaneously. Do not turn off the computer or remove disks while a program is executing and the disks are running, or you may damage the disks.

RECOVERING FROM SYSTEM FAILURE

Suspect the operator first:

1. Check the mechanical items:

   - Are all cables attached, with no loose connections?
   - Are all cables in the correct place?

2. Did you give the correct command?

   - Remove disks and turn everything off.

- Turn the computer on.
- Repeat the command.

3. Make sure that you are using the correct program and that the program you are trying to use is present on the disk you are using.

Suspect the disk next:

4. Use a fresh disk if it is a floppy. The current disk may have been damaged.

    - Use a backup disk. Do not use any program on your current disk.
    - If no backup exists, take the time to make one.

Check the software:

5. Make sure that you are using the correct programs:

    - Do you have the correct DOS version?
    - Are you using the correct application program?

The DOS Control Characters

Command	Action
Esc	Cancel line
ˆ Break (ˆC)	Terminates program
ˆ NumLock (ˆS)	Freezes screen
ˆ PrtSc (ˆP)	Engages or disengages printer
Shift-PrtSc	Prints information on screen
Del (ˆG)	Deletes character at cursor position
Backspace (ˆH)	Deletes character to left of cursor
ˆZ	Marks end of string in COPY

C The ASCII Characters and the Extended ASCII Characters

The ASCII characters (the first page) and the extended ASCII characters (the second page) are identified by the numbers 1 to 255. The number of a given character is the sum of its row and column numbers. For example, the letter A has a value of 65 (64 + 1) and the upper-right corner for a box is 191 (176 + 15).

Character Set (00–7F) Quick Reference

DECIMAL VALUE ➡	⬇	0	16	32	48	64	80	96	112
⬇	HEXA DECIMAL VALUE	0	1	2	3	4	5	6	7
0	0	BLANK (NULL)	►	BLANK (SPACE)	0	@	P	'	p
1	1	☺	◄	!	1	A	Q	a	q
2	2	☻	↕	''	2	B	R	b	r
3	3	♥	‼	#	3	C	S	c	s
4	4	♦	¶	$	4	D	T	d	t
5	5	♣	§	%	5	E	U	e	u
6	6	♠	▬	&	6	F	V	f	v
7	7	•	↨	'	7	G	W	g	w
8	8	◘	↑	(	8	H	X	h	x
9	9	○	↓	)	9	I	Y	i	y
10	A	◎	→	*	:	J	Z	j	z
11	B	♂	←	+	;	K	[	k	{
12	C	♀	∟	,	<	L	\	l	¦
13	D	♪	↔	—	=	M	]	m	}
14	E	♫	▲	.	>	N	∧	n	~
15	F	☼	▼	/	?	O	_	o	△

Character Set (88–FF) Quick Reference

DECIMAL VALUE →	HEXADECIMAL VALUE →	128 / 8	144 / 9	160 / A	176 / B	192 / C	208 / D	224 / E	240 / F
0	0	Ç	É	á	▓	└	╨	∝	≡
1	1	ü	æ	í	▒	┴	╤	β	±
2	2	é	Æ	ó	▓	┬	╥	Γ	≥
3	3	â	ô	ú	│	├	╙	π	≤
4	4	ä	ö	ñ	┤	─	╘	Σ	∫
5	5	à	ò	Ñ	╡	┼	╒	σ	∫
6	6	å	û	ª	╢	╞	╓	µ	÷
7	7	ç	ù	º	╖	╟	╫	τ	≈
8	8	ê	ÿ	¿	╕	╚	╪	Φ	°
9	9	ë	Ö	⌐	╣	╔	┘	θ	•
10	A	è	Ü	¬	║	╩	┌	Ω	•
11	B	ï	¢	½	╗	╦	█	δ	√
12	C	î	£	¼	╝	╠	█	∞	n
13	D	ì	¥	¡	╜	═	█	φ	²
14	E	Ä	₧	«	╛	╬	█	∈	∎
15	F	Å	ƒ	»	┐	╧	█	∩	BLANK FF

Technical Reference Manual, pp.7-12–7-13, © 1984 International Business Machines Corporation

Index

Kilobytes, 3

Label, disk, 37
LABEL program, 134–135, 197
LOCATE program, 123–127

Main memory, 3, 12
MD (Make Directory) command, 90, 197
Memory
  main, 3, 12
  size, 3
Memory-resident programs. *See* SideKick and SuperKey
MKDIR command. *See* MD (Make Directory) command
MODE program, 128–129, 198
Monochrome screen, 5
MORE program, 134, 200
MS-DOS. *See* DOS

NULL option, 103, 111

Parameters, file-name, 47–52, 129, 131
Partitioning hard disks, 84–86, 104–106
PATH command, 96–97, 103, 201–203
PC-DOS. *See* DOS
Ports, 12, 198–199
Printer, 218
  engaging, 21–22
  types of, 6
Printing files, 59–61, 151
PRN, 60, 111
PROMPT command, 94–95, 203–205

RAM disk, 12, 99, 103–104
RD (Remove Directory) command, 205
Read-only files, 9–10, 120–122, 151, 182–184

Redirection, 58–60, 111
RENAME command, 114–116, 205
RMDIR command. *See* RD (Remove Directory) command

Scrolling, 21, 111
Search path, 96–97, 103
SET command, 104, 206
Shift keys, 4
SideKick, 155–180
  activating, 156
  ASCII table, 178
  block commands, 167–168
  calculator, 174–177
  calendar, 177–178
  cutting and pasting, 172–174
  deleting text in, 166–168
  exiting, 161
  expanding files in, 163–164
  find and replace commands, 164–166
  hot key, 160
  importing, 172–174
  inserting text with, 166–167
  installing, 158–160
  loading from AUTOEXEC.BAT, 170–171
  moving cursor in, 162–163
  notepad, 162–170
  pasting, 172–174
  removing, 161
  saving files in, 169
  selecting features, 161
  sorting with, 168–170
  transferring to disks, 156
Software, 1, 13–14
Sorting,
  with SORT program, 52–55, 127, 201, 206
  with SideKick, 168–170
Starting up your computer, 16–17
Subdirectories, 27, 89–94
  listing, 126–128
  sorting, 52–55, 127
SUBST program, 207

SYBEX Computer Books
are different.

Here is why . . .

At SYBEX, each book is designed with you in mind. Every manuscript is carefully selected and supervised by our editors, who are themselves computer experts. We publish the best authors, whose technical expertise is matched by an ability to write clearly and to communicate effectively. Programs are thoroughly tested for accuracy by our technical staff. Our computerized production department goes to great lengths to make sure that each book is well-designed.

In the pursuit of timeliness, SYBEX has achieved many publishing firsts. SYBEX was among the first to integrate personal computers used by authors and staff into the publishing process. SYBEX was the first to publish books on the CP/M operating system, microprocessor interfacing techniques, word processing, and many more topics.

Expertise in computers and dedication to the highest quality product have made SYBEX a world leader in computer book publishing. Translated into fourteen languages, SYBEX books have helped millions of people around the world to get the most from their computers. We hope we have helped you, too.

For a complete catalog of our publications:

SYBEX, Inc. 2021 Challenger Drive, #100, Alameda, CA 94501
Tel: (415) 523-8233/(800) 227-2346   Telex: 336311